A random physicist takes on economics

A personal view by Jason Smith

A Random Physicist Takes on Economics by Jason Smith. Published by arandomphysicist.

www.arandomphysicist.com

contact@arandomphysicist.com

ISBN: 9781549599231

Cover by Jason Smith

Introduction

I am a random physicist. If you were to select at random a physics PhD from the population of the United States, you'd probably end up with someone like me. I went to two large state schools (The University of Texas and the University of Washington). I am a male in field with an over-representation of males (like economics). Like most physicists, I didn't pursue an academic career. Instead I ended up working in the defense and aerospace sector.

One way that I'm not typical is that I was a theoretical physicist (the ones writing the equations) as opposed to an experimental physicist (the ones running the experiments) — there are many more of the latter. My field was nuclear and particle physics — my thesis was titled "Quarks and antiquarks in nuclei" if that gives you a flavor.

As I was finishing up that thesis and deciding against going into academia, I looked around at my other options. This was 2004 and the big thing physicists were doing in the real world was building financial models on Wall Street — if "real" is the appropriate adjective. I looked into becoming what they call a "quant". I studied some quantitative finance. I had a couple interviews. I was offered a job at what I'll call Major Financial Company (MFC) helping to develop mortgage risk models in 2005, but (luckily, it turns out) I turned it down. However this is when my interest in economics started. It was also the heyday of the economics blog on the Internet.

Instead, I took a research and development position in signal processing which for professional reasons will go by the name of Large Defense Contractor (LDC). At its most basic level signal processing the study of methods of extracting meaningful information from data. There's a new term out there for people who do this with enormous data sets called a "data scientist". That's not what I do. I stick to smaller data sets.

At this point in my life it looked like economics was in the rear-view mirror, but that changed after two events. First, the biggest financial crisis since the Great Depression hit in 2008. I was glad I didn't take that job; MFC went bankrupt. However, the economics blogs were inundated with all kinds of explanations, criticisms of economics, and claims of predictions. I asked myself: How could I tell if any particular economic theory was adding value?

Second, LDC sponsored me for a government fellowship in 2011 which temporarily relocated me to Washington, DC. I was introduced to some research into the use of prediction markets for intelligence problems as part of the Intelligence Advanced Research Projects Activity (IARPA) Aggregative Contingent Estimation (ACE) program. I actually participated in the Decomposition-Based Elicitation and Aggregation (DAGGRE) project as a test participant, which was a forerunner of the now-defunct SciCast.

Prediction markets are a kind of options market that lets you place a bet on an outcome. You have option contracts that, for example, would pay $1 if Hillary Clinton won the 2016 US Presidential election. If you thought that wasn't going to happen, one of those contracts is worth close to zero for you. If you thought it was definitely going to happen, it would have been worth closer to $1 to you. With enough people participating in the prediction market, the value will be somewhere in between — say $0.70. If you thought Clinton had a better than 70% chance, you'd likely make money if you bought at that price (or higher). If you were holding a contract and you thought Clinton had a worse than 70% chance, you could have sold at the market rate (or lower). For intelligence prediction markets, those options contracts would be for events like whether Iran will test a nuclear weapon in the next year.

The first time I had ever encountered prediction markets was during the 2004 presidential election (via the Iowa Electronic Markets). Research has shown that prediction markets do just about as well as polls. This actually makes them advantageous over polls in one sense; prediction markets are asynchronous polls like those dials given to focus groups as they watch debates these days. One weird property of prediction markets are sudden shifts in the market price — almost as if a wave of new conventional wisdom sweeps over the participants. While these markets seemed like a new form of polling in regards to elections (regardless of what their proponents' advocacy says), it could be problematic in the world of intelligence. We had already seen herding behavior in intelligence without prediction markets in the run-up to the Iraq War and the 2008 financial crisis wasn't exactly a big point in favor of markets in general. You could have made a killing shorting Clinton in 2016 in online prediction markets. I had a serious question: *How could we tell if prediction markets are working?*

One of my proposed solutions to find out if prediction markets were working was to try to check the performance of a prediction market against a random person (in economics jargon, "agent") model. Assign people random probabilities they believe an event will occur known only to them (a random valuation of an options contract as private information), and let them randomly encounter each other to trade. If the distribution of final options contract payouts was consistent with empirical data from prediction markets and was directly related to the initial random distribution of probabilities (valuations), then the real information is in that initial probability distribution. If a model with random agents could explain prediction market results, then prediction markets really aren't much more than polls of that initial probability distribution. The relevant information is in the initial probability distribution, not the series of transactions and prices.

Of course that is just a test of the "information aggregation" mechanism — aggregating that private information (each agent's private event probabilities) into the overall probability distribution. There's another important piece of prediction markets: the ability to reward (with money) high quality knowledge and punish (by losing money) low quality knowledge (or errors). If they are functioning correctly in theory, prediction markets act as a one-way valve pumping good knowledge in and bad knowledge out. That would take a bit more theoretical work to understand.

Incidentally, around the same time both of these questions came up in my head, I discovered by a short preprint by physicists Peter Fielitz and Guenter Borchardt at arXiv.org (a repository for pre-publication physics and other technical papers) while looking for references about a signal processing topic called compressed sensing. Its title (at the time) was "Information transfer model of natural processes". It was in the general physics (gen-ph) section. The first line of the abstract tells the basic story:

> *Information theory provides shortcuts which allow [one] to deal with complex systems.*

The paper is an attempt to answer a technical question about applying the so-called principle of maximum entropy expounded by Edwin Jaynes in 1957 in situations when you don't have things like the conservation of energy that you have in physics. Markets are complex systems — and there aren't conservation laws like conservation of energy in economics; I saw in this paper the potential to answer my questions about prediction markets and economic theory.

I was temporarily relocated in Washington, DC, in a long distance relationship with my future wife, with few friends in the area, and lots of time outside of work on my hands so I dove in. I tried to work out how to couch the concepts of supply and demand as well as the price mechanism in this very simple theoretical framework. I later started thinking out loud on a blog. Peter Fielitz and Guenter Borchardt eventually updated their preprint with a new title ("A general concept of natural information equilibrium") and to reference to "non-physical ... economical processes" along with my blog. Peter

Fielitz got in touch with me and we have an ongoing discussion about concept of information equilibrium. I eventually put up a preprint myself in the quantitative finance economics (q-fin.EC) section of arXiv.org titled "Information equilibrium as an economic principle".

I showed some of the early results to Jason Matheny at IARPA in a pitch for funding to see if it might be a useful way to produce metrics for prediction markets. He was very encouraging, but told me that I should put it in front of some academic economists. I tried to publish my preprint in an economics journal, but that resulted in immediate desk rejections. A desk rejection is where a paper is rejected before even going to peer review (based on the title and author's name and affiliation, I guess). I can't say I blame them — economics journals probably receive a choice selection of the collective id's theories of money. There are a lot of crackpot theories about economics out there, and I try to remind myself of physicist Sean Carroll's "The Alternative-Science Respectability Checklist" blog post from June of 2007 to keep from starting down the dark path.

A version of the information equilibrium model paper from Fielitz and Borchardt was published in Physics Essays as "A generalized concept of information transfer". However the material in my paper hasn't gone through peer review yet, so I'm not going to talk about it very much. It covers the technical application of the principles I am going to talk about here to economic systems — and actually comes up with many of the same results as standard economics but without a lot of the additional assumptions about rational behavior (to give one example). Luckily David Glasner, an economist at the Federal Trade Commission and in my opinion one of the best economics bloggers on the Internet, recognized some of my arguments as very similar to ones advanced by economist and Nobel laureate Gary Becker in 1962 in a paper titled "Irrational Behavior and Economic Theory". It is from that starting point that I will take on economics.

I know that lots of people out there are probably saying to themselves: *A physicist? Oh, no! There are going to be a lot of equations!* Math is a tool, but I've been working with these topics for long enough that I can (hopefully) explain them in plain language. It used to be that economics was discussed with long dry prose, with occasional snappy political tracts (even a graphic novel of sorts made from Friedrich Hayek's *The Road to Serfdom*). Even John Maynard Keynes' seminal *The General Theory of Employment, Interest and Money* (hereafter, *The General Theory*) only has a few equations among its hundreds of pages.

* * *

I going to add some notes before we begin. If you are familiar with economics jargon, you can probably safely skip to the next chapter. I'm not going to be too formal about citations, but plan to give credit where it's due. I'll cite articles by authors, title and year but keep it within the narrative. Everything here is discoverable on the internet.

I will refer to a "Nobel Memorial Prize in Economic Sciences" as a Nobel Prize and a winners as a Nobel laureate. It doesn't matter that Alfred Nobel didn't choose economics as a field to be honored; it matters that people today generally think of the prize as if he did. As it will occasionally be used as a sarcastic honorific, sticklers for detail should be satisfied.

Economics is divided into two broad fields: microeconomics and macroeconomics (maybe three if you consider growth economics). Economics has basically become the general study of systems that involve money, although it has branched out to include cases where people make strategic decisions of any kind (via game theory, and the work of the aforementioned Gary Becker). *Macro-* is a prefix that is used to mean the system is large — macroeconomics is the economics of nations. This is what many people think of when it comes to talk of "the economy" in our daily lives. Microeconomics is the economics of individuals. In physics we use these terms as well and sometimes we talk about micro theories and macro theories — typically in reference to theories at small scales (like particles) versus large scales (like gravity). In between, we have the mesoscale.

Beyond macro and micro (and meso), there's some more economics jargon that appears often enough to warrant a glossary. Other terms are less frequently referenced and will be defined where they appear.

Agent: A generic term for the thing in an economic model that is doing stuff. It could be an individual person, a "household" or a firm (a business). In physics, we tend to refer to this as a "degree of freedom", although an agent would probably represent more than one degree of freedom. An atom usually represents at least six degrees of freedom (3D movement/momentum and 3D location). Another physics term would be the "particle content" of a quantum field theory. Quantum electrodynamics (QED) is made up of electrons and photons — those are the "agents" in the QED model.

Central bank: A national bank that has some (metaphorical) levers that ostensibly control the value of money and/or interest rates. The United States has the Federal Reserve System (called the "Fed"), which has a chairperson (in 2017 it is Janet Yellen, who has been in office since 2014). In the UK, they have the Bank of England. In Japan, they have the Bank of Japan. In New Zealand, they have the Reserve Bank of New Zealand. You get the picture.

DSGE: In the aftermath of the global financial crisis, this has become a four-letter word. It stands for Dynamic Stochastic General Equilibrium, and represents the general mathematical framework used by most of macroeconomics. When critics claim the models didn't predict the financial crisis, they are probably referring to DSGE models which typically have a strong tendency to return to an economy in "equilibrium". The truth is that this approach is actually pretty general, and some DSGE model can probably describe the macroeconomy pretty well. The issue is that specific standard implementations (that include things like the empirically questionable Euler equation describing how agents balance the present and future) tend to be no better than simple random autoregressive stochastic processes at forecasting. Macroeconomists have been hard at work questioning their foundations and adding financial sectors, but as quality macroeconomic data is somewhat limited these complex models can't really be confirmed or rejected.

Expectations: Agents' views of the future. There are different models for how expectations are formed (or learned). They can be backward-looking (based on history) or forward-looking (based on tea leaves and Tarot cards). If you think inflation is going to raise prices by a few percent in the next year, that's your inflation expectation. A better word would really be beliefs, but that has a different meaning in economics. As it is, the term collides with the physics and math term "expectation value", which is a more general form of an average. In a lot of economics, expectations are the most powerful force in the economic universe. No, really.

Fiscal policy: Passionately hated by some elements of the political sphere since John Maynard Keynes said it was a good idea for macroeconomic stabilization policy, this consists of the general taxation and spending decisions by the central government (in the US, bills passed by Congress and not vetoed by the President). It includes "automatic stabilizers" like unemployment insurance and temporary measures like the American Recovery and Reinvestment Act of 2009, also known as the Obama stimulus. Despite what you hear in the media and from politicians, most economists (in surveys) think it is useful to mitigate the effects of a recession in combination with monetary policy.

Homo economicus: A play on the binomial nomenclature Carl Linnaeus developed for biology. Real humans are *Homo sapiens*; rational utility maximizing agents are a very different species called *Homo economicus*.

Inflation: The rate of change of the price level. It measures how fast prices are rising. Ever since the the dawn of money, people have worried about inflation. It was apparently bad in the 1970s. For a lot of people, the music that happened when they were young is the best music. For economists, the inflation rate that happened when they were young is the natural tendency for inflation. Our current set of establishment figures contains a lot of people who were young in the 1970s, so naturally a lot of policy is averse to inflation. Additionally, there is no universally accepted textbook economic theory of what causes inflation. The closest thing to such a theory is the idea that it is set by monetary policy, but there are still multiple possible mechanisms.

Price level: A kind of average price for everything in the economy. In the United States we hear about the Consumer Price Index (or CPI) in the news. In the European Union, they have the Harmonized Index of Consumer Prices (HICP). "Core" CPI tends to leave out food and energy, which fluctuate a lot (so month to month numbers are unreliable indicators of where inflation is going). There are all kinds of adjustments made to accommodate things that didn't used to exist like iPhones, or last longer than they used to like cars. The US has another price level called the Personal Consumption Expenditures (PCE) index that some people (including the Fed) think is better than CPI. The two measures generally say about the same thing (PCE changes a bit slower).

Maximizing: When rational agents are trying to get the best deal for themselves, they're maximizing some objective. When translated into mathematics, this objective becomes an objective function (such as utility, see below). For example, in the song "Money, Power, Glory" Lana del Rey expresses a desire to maximize those three things (ironically in my interpretation, but maybe not).

Monetary policy: Generally the actions of the central bank that purportedly guide the economy. Sometimes (especially by non-economists) referred to as "printing money", this is not exactly what happens — a point you cannot avoid hearing about at length if you've spent any time on economics blogs. Most economists (in surveys) think this is massively important, but the big exception is the so-called "liquidity trap" which is a macroeconomic condition where some economists think (standard) monetary policy doesn't help mitigate a recession.

Money: You might think there is a generally accepted textbook theory of what money is (say, cash) and how it works in the economy, but there isn't. There are several different aggregate measures of money in an economy with names like M1, M2, and M3. When measuring printed notes and minted coins ("M0") started to fail to conform to then-fashionable economic theory, M1 was invented. When M1 stopped conforming to theory, M2 was invented. Today we still have most of these measures. M0 is added together with accounts private banks have at the central bank (see above) to create something called the "monetary base". Different economists have different opinions on these measures, with many discounting them altogether. Milton Friedman was a strong proponent of controlling M2 to control inflation at one point. Non-economists sometimes have extremely strong opinions about these measures for reasons that I don't quite understand.

Nominal: A retronym for money amounts that aren't adjusted for inflation. Because we now have "real dollars", we have to have "nominal dollars" when we just used to say "dollars". It's like the terms "cloth diaper" and "acoustic guitar".

Rational: This means lots of different things to different people, but most commonly in economics just two. Rational agents try to get the best deal for themselves they can, and don't make mistakes on average. Rational expectations (or model-consistent expectations) is a very specific model of expectations where the expected value of something like inflation is what inflation actually is in the model in the future. In physics, we refer to a dependency on a future value of the time coordinate as either "advanced" or more often "causality violating".

Real: Dollar, yen, or pounds sterling (etc) amounts adjusted for inflation. When Dr. Evil in *Austin Powers* requests a ransom of one million dollars, the joke is that he forgot to adjust for inflation since the 1960s (which would be about $5 million dollars in the 1990s). The real joke is on us because the drastic rise in income inequality since the 1960s requires Dr. Evil has to ask for $100 billion dollars since he represents the top 1%.

Recession: It is actually kind of funny to try to give a definition of a recession because there really isn't one. There's a general idea of a macroeconomic "business cycle" (of which a recession is one piece) out there, but it's not really cyclic in the sense of a regular cycle. One aspect of recessions that is pretty robust is that unemployment goes up. A heuristic some use is two consecutive quarters of negative Gross Domestic Product (GDP) growth. They used to be called depressions until the Great Depression of the 1930s. Like how NOAA retires hurricane names when they're bad enough, the word *depression* is now generally avoided in favor of *recession*. Who knows? Maybe the so-called Great Recession of 2008-2009 may lead to retiring the term *recession*. Anyway, economists have no consensus definition of what a recession is or how to react to one. An economist's personal definition of a recession is a good indicator for the kind of macroeconomic models and theories that economist subscribes to. The majority of economists (in surveys) think a combination of monetary and fiscal policy is the best way to mitigate recessions.

Representative agent: A model simplification where all the agents are basically the same. If you think that sounds strange in a field where the main idea is that I have blueberries and you have money so we do a swap, you're right.

Utility: Instead of Lana del Rey's objective function, economists tend to combine money, power, glory, happiness, health, and many more "good things" into a single measure of goodness called utility. If you've ever taken a philosophy course on ethical theories, you've probably heard of the moral system centered on Jeremy Bentham called Utilitarianism. The conflation of economics and ethical philosophy has been with us ever since.

Zero-sum: A term derived from game theory where essentially one player's win is another player's loss. This is common heuristic used by people when it comes to economics especially with regard to immigration and trade despite the fact that the empirical data shows that both are generally positive-sum — they benefit everyone.

The critique

The aftermath of the global financial crisis has become an exciting time in the field of political economy. In the UK, university economics students demanded changes to the curriculum calling for pluralism in the teaching of economics. In Bristol, businesses and individuals set up a "local currency" called Bristol Pounds. The Occupy Wall Street movement set up small barter economies while objecting to major financial institutions receiving bailouts from the federal government in contrast to the fact that people who had recently graduated or were still in college had to pay off their student loans despite a lack of jobs exacerbated by the excessive leverage of those same financial institutions. Apps have been developed to facilitate gift-exchange economies. There was a self-declared socialist running for President of the United States (who did pretty well), and a broad based movement to effectively double the minimum wage to $15. The Republicans abandoned their previous dedication to free markets, advocating trade protectionism and intervention. In many places, the perceived failure of economic theory in the financial crisis has opened the door to "populist" zero-sum economic theories replacing hard lessons of the Great Depression. In fact, the most sensible take on our current economic situation is based on the economic theories of the 1930s, with more modern theories either throwing up their arms or belatedly struggling to add financial sectors to their models. The time seems right to improve the economics that has become a consensus view not just among economists themselves, but the political elite. Most paradigm shifts in economics come with major economic crises; a prime example is the Keynesian economics following the Great Depression of the 1930s.

In addition to the social and political stirrings (or possibly the cause of them), there has been increasing criticism of the major institutions in charge of the direction of the economy. Central banks and central governments, the sources of monetary and fiscal policy, have been embarking on policies considered experimental or even ill-advised. Several governments have experimented with so-called "austerity" policies — cutbacks in government spending, including programs for the poor — against the advice of mainstream economists.

Central banks have attempted policies such as quantitative easing and negative interest rates that while in line with mainstream economic theories have not resulted in much evidence they have accomplished their goals. The key "evidence" seems to be the "counterfactual": what didn't happen according to those same economics theories. The claim is that the US economy would have been much worse without the trillions of dollars of quantitative easing. I am not saying this isn't true, but I am saying that it is hard as a scientist to accept a conclusion where you have to believe the theory in order to both recommend the policy and know if it worked. In the case of the Fed's quantitative easing program, the data is perfectly consistent with the result that it did nothing except lower short term interest rates to nearly zero.

And if the experimental policies weren't a big enough subject to criticize, three of the biggest economies in the world (the United States, the European Union and Japan ... and even a few of the smaller economies) keep missing their central banks' forecasts. Since macroeconomics teaches that central banks generally control the variables in those forecasts, such as inflation and interest rates, this poses a bit of a problem.

Now it is true that if I am late to every appointment I make, I am in some sense not meeting a forecast I control. We'd say that my appointments are not credible. And that is one of the ways modern economics explains persistent undershooting of inflation in many advanced countries in the aftermath of the Global Financial Crisis. But this raises odd questions such as why New Zealand's central bank is credible while the US Federal Reserve Bank is not. Would the Fed become credible if we replaced the Federal Reserve Open Market Committee (FOMC) with the equivalent personnel from New Zealand? Would swapping Graeme Wheeler with Janet Yellen suffice?

It's possible that if you keep forecasting rain and it doesn't happen, you might not control the weather. Humans have a natural tendency to believe in our own agency. Many people think the President of the United States has control over the economy. Economists laugh and say that's ridiculous — it's the leadership at the Fed that controls the economy most of the time. The New York Times relates an anecdote in a piece titled "America's Endless War Over Money" from 2015 that reflects both of these views:

> *And in 1965, President Lyndon B. Johnson, who wanted cheap credit to finance the Vietnam War and his Great Society, summoned Fed chairman William McChesney Martin to his Texas ranch. There, after asking other officials to leave the room, Johnson reportedly shoved Martin against the wall as he demanding that the Fed once again hold down interest rates. Martin caved, the Fed printed money, and inflation kept climbing until the early 1980s.*

That must have been some shove for it to have had an effect on inflation for the next 15 years, 10 of which Martin wasn't even in office. Additionally, interest rates went up after 1965. We humans like to tell stories like this. "Great men" (it has almost always been men in these stories in this field) change the course of the economy. Paul Volcker, Fed chairperson from 1979 to 1987, is credited with "breaking the back" of the high inflation of the 1970s. Alan Greenspan, Fed chairperson from 1987 to 2006, is credited with the so-called Great Moderation — a period of relative macroeconomic stability lasting from 1987 until 2008.

Human agency is at the heart of economics, whether it is in leadership positions at central banks or individuals making decisions in free markets. Additionally, free markets and economic approaches to cost-benefit calculations have become a default position that has reached into every political party and venue: cap and trade for lowering greenhouse gasses; the earned income tax credit (EITC) for fighting poverty; higher marginal tax rates for economic inequality. Is economics as a field up to the importance of the policy questions it addresses? Is it (empirically or theoretically) correct enough? Can it be? In this book, I hope to convince you that the answer is: *No, at least not yet.*

There is an odd defense of the lack of empirical success in economics. It is argued that it is a branch of logic or philosophy (famously by Keynes in a 1938 letter to Roy Harrod) and therefore does not have to conform to empirical data. However, there are some economic models that do explain empirical data. Choosing which models to shield from data and which models not to shield is problematic. Any model that fails empirically could just be argued to not have to succeed empirically. In fact, Nobel laureate and economist Edward Prescott has argued that exact line of defense in his 2016 paper "RBC Methodology and the Development of Aggregate Economic Theory" where he writes:

> *Reality is complex, and any model economy used is necessarily an abstraction and therefore false. This does not mean, however, that model economies are not useful in drawing scientific inference.*

A field where one of its highest honors has been bestowed on someone who writes statements like this has a serious problem with empirical reality. This is of course true in a simple sense: models are always useful, but all models have to show some ability to explain observations and data, not just in proving the postulates of the model itself.

It is true that — in a neat example of supply and demand — the value economic criticism has dropped significantly due to over-supply in the post-financial crisis world. I hope my critiques are novel, but where they are not I hope they are more nuanced and constructive. For example, there are many critiques of the way mathematics used in economics, but few come from people with a physicist's belief in the power of mathematics —

and even fewer of those ask for a change toward simpler mathematical models. Despite my critiques, I also defend several modern economic concepts frequently attacked from rational utility maximization (probably a good effective theory near equilibrium) to DSGE models (as noted already, probably general enough framework to provide a correct description of an economy).

My critiques do not mean we should abandon the purely statistical models, experience and stylized facts that make up the institutional knowledge academic economics departments, central banks and central governments, nor the empirical microeconomics and behavioral economics studies that form the basis of any possibility of understanding. Actually, I am making a case that is all we should keep.

* * *

So what questions form the basis of my critique?

I question the use of overly-formal math in economics. There are serious problems with formalization and disconnection from physical reality to such a degree that I am not convinced economists think the math they use is supposed to have a connection to physical reality and empirical data. As a physicist, I am no stranger to the "unreasonable effectiveness of mathematics"

(Eugene Wigner, 1960). However, there is usually a proportional relationship between the mathematical complexity of the theory and the empirical accuracy of that theory. When George Box told us that "all models are wrong" in 1976, he was advising against using overly-complex models unless they explain data extremely accurately. Modern economic theory (and especially macroeconomic theory) has ignored this advice and constructs models of such formal complexity that I was surprised to hear they fail to provide better forecasts than simple autoregressive stochastic processes or linear extrapolation.

I question the role of human agency in economics. I am asking economics to question a principle it has held onto for literally hundreds of years. The people involved in buying and selling may not be as important as the shape of the realm of possibilities of that buying and selling. Economic agents — firms, households, individuals — might just be a one way to explore that realm. However, a drop of cream in coffee also "explores" its realm of possibilities. If something in economics arises from simply the ability to explore the opportunity set, it becomes a fair question as to whether that result is due to the agents or the opportunity set.

I question the role of expectations in economics. If you have ever read, listened to or watched business news, you will be familiar with market expectations. Company ABC's stock can tumble if their earnings don't meet "the Street's" expectations. In the hands of economists, these expectations become a way for changes in the future to impact the present and allow them to explain literally any possible result.

I question the understanding of so-called sticky prices in economics. This may seem like a small technical issue, but in macroeconomics, one way to get monetary policy (the decisions of the Federal Reserve, or "the Fed") to have any effect on the economy is through sticky (i.e. hard to budge, also called "rigid") prices and wages. Wages are frequently considered just another price (the price of labor). Therefore sticky prices are a linchpin for much of the modern macroeconomic framework — pull it out, and the edifice might come down. The problem is that individual prices do not appear to actually be sticky.

I question how agents are combined into an economy. Economists have brushed aside a significant result in their field since the 1970s called the Sonnenschein-Mantel-Debreu (SMD) theorem. The work-around that there is just one person, one representative agent, cannot begin to capture major impacts of coordination among different agents or their differing forecasts of the future.

I question the interpretation of the price mechanism. One modern view is that a price represents an aggregation of economic agents' knowledge about a subject. That is the key to prediction markets: they are an implementation of the idea that everyone has a little piece of information about the real state of the world, and if you make it possible to trade on that information, all the information becomes available to everybody through the price. You probably find it hard to believe you can gather up all the different kinds of information about blueberry yields, rainfall, the number of farmers, their experience at blueberry farming, and so on, and represent it as a single number in a useful way. I do, too. A price is, however, pretty useful for understanding what it takes to buy blueberries so the price mechanism does represent a useful tool in understanding the allocation of scarce resources.

I question the place economics has relative to the social sciences. From the previous questions, you can probably see a trend towards removing a lot of human agency from economic theory. After looking at this problem for several years, I find that most of the things that economics is successful at describing have little to do with human agency. And the things it is terrible at describing (there is no agreed on idea of what a recession is in economics) may be the result of our human qualities (a tendency to panic together) that have nothing to do with money. In that sense, economics may be simply the study of functioning markets, while the study of recessions and market failures may be the domain of psychology, sociology and neuroscience. In *A Tract on Monetary Reform*, John Maynard Keynes famously said:

> *In the long run we are all dead. Economists set themselves too easy, too useless a task, if in tempestuous seasons they can only tell us, that when the storm is long past, the ocean is flat again.*

* * *

In addition to delivering these critiques, I also wanted to take my basic arguments to the public. Economics is being used to motivate public policy decisions, and so the public should be aware of what economics says — not just what economists say economics says.

Normally, I'd be sympathetic to the idea of experts in a field explaining that field to the public. The implicit assumption behind this is that something external enforces discipline on the field. For example, most scientific fields have empirical data and experiments. Unfortunately, for a lot of economics, the theory turns out to be either wrong or inconclusive when compared to data. For example, in a 2011 paper Rochelle Edge and Refet Gurkaynak found that formally complex DSGE models are very poor at forecasting.

And since so much of economic theory is couched in unnecessarily complex mathematics (unnecessary because the theory being presented doesn't explain empirical data), a lot of the arguments are difficult to wade through even for someone who completed a course on string theory (e.g. me). The terse math probably is a consequence of the view that economics is a branch of logic. For example, reading through economics papers, I frequently come across a reference to a variable being a member of the set of "positive real numbers" by its mathematical symbol, a kind of stylized chalk board version of a bold capital letter R, no less. I have no idea what advantage that confers over "a number greater than zero", especially when the model in question does not explain empirical data. When economist Paul Romer (now Chief Economist at the World Bank) wrote a paper titled "Mathiness in the Theory of Economic Growth" in 2015, I initially thought "mathiness" might have referred to this kind of nonsense. Turns out that isn't the case (and Romer was actually complaining about the opposite problem of not enough of those R's — more on that later).

While some economists do a great job when it comes to explaining theories to the public (Nobel laureate Paul Krugman comes to mind), others resort to distorted "Economics 101" reasoning even when it doesn't apply — which includes most macroeconomic situations — out of political expediency. The latter is well documented in James Kwak's *Economism* (2017). I've now spent several years engaged in this world; I hope my own attempt to navigate it is useful to others. I've tried to understand it using the tools I have — scaling arguments and assuming something is random if it is beyond my understanding. That last bit is important. Something that is extraordinarily complex can be indistinguishable from something that is random. In fact in complexity theory, algorithmic randomness is the upper limit of algorithmic complexity.

Physicists

There is really nothing more pathetic than to have an economist or a retired engineer try to force analogies between the concepts of physics and the concepts of economics. How many dreary papers have I had to referee in which the author is looking for something that corresponds to entropy or to one or another form of energy. Nonsensical laws, such as the law of conservation of purchasing power, represent spurious social science imitations of the important physical law of the conservation of energy; and when an economist makes reference to a Heisenberg Principle of indeterminacy in the social world, at best this must be regarded as a figure of speech or a play on words, rather than a valid application of the relations of quantum mechanics.

That is Paul Samuelson: economist, Nobel laureate, and considered one of the parents of modern economics. He wrote it in an article titled "Maximum Principles in Analytical Economics" in 1970. This quote is somewhat ironic, though, because what Samuelson did for economics was basically import a lot of math developed to solve physics problems into economics.

Irving Fisher, another one of the leading lights of mathematical economics had his 1892 thesis supervised by the physicist (and chemist, and mathematician ...) Willard Gibbs, who along with Ludwig Boltzmann developed statistical mechanics. I imagine this is the twin birth of mathematical economics and what would eventually be dubbed econophysics (loosely, the study of economics using statistical mechanics techniques). Physics — or at least its methodology — is everywhere in economics.

I think this is a touchy subject. Another economist, Chris House, asked in a blog post from March 21, 2014 titled "Why Are Physicists Drawn to Economics?" ... well, *Why are physicists drawn to economics?* In it, House claims that physicists think they are better at math — or think they have different techniques that will be useful — and so think they can jump right in. It's an example of the so-called Dunning-Kruger effect (after psychologists David Dunning and Justin Kruger): people who don't know anything about a subject are the worst people to assess their capabilities in that subject.

I can tell you why this physicist jumped right in, and it has nothing to do with math, but with data. Physicists are used to seeing graphs of theoretical (i.e. mathematical) curves going through sets of data points with error bars (to represent theoretical and/or experimental error). These graphs are a distillation of what physicists *know*. I am using *know* here in a specific sense: we *know* something if there is general agreement that the theory that produces those curves isn't rejected by the data. In that case, we know something. It may not be much, but it's something.

After several years of searching through papers, reading a couple of introductory economics textbooks, and eventually reading a couple of graduate school level textbooks on macroeconomics, this never seems to happen. There are very few graphs of theoretical curves going through data.

So I imagine the typical physicist starts looking at economics, sees Lagrange multiplier problems but almost never data, and arrives at the conclusion: these people don't *know* anything. If they did, there would be at least a couple of graphs of theoretical curves going through data points. Physicists don't think they're better at math. They grasp the basics of the math in economics. They just think the field of economics is wide open to new theories, due to the paucity of theoretical models that explain measured data.

House also claims that physicists aren't actually better at math. This might be right: the math scores on the Graduate Record Exam (GRE, required for a lot of graduate schools in the United States) tend to be about the same for the two fields. Economists and physicists are probably equally good at the mechanics of math. But this claim is also wrong when it comes to a very important issue I hope to make clear: applied math is supposed to represent some kind of physical or economic reality. It's probably because physicists have those theoretical curves going through experimental data that makes them better at grasping this.

I'm going to illustrate this with a story involving the economist Paul Romer I mentioned earlier. Romer made a splash in the economics community in 2015 where he lamented "mathiness" in economics papers. I won't go too much into his definition of "mathiness", but suffice to say it is a pejorative term for work that isn't sufficiently strict about its equations. Romer attempts to capture the economists Robert Lucas and Benjamin Moll in an act of mathiness. It is important to note that beyond this specific act of mathiness, Romer disagrees with the general approach advocated by Lucas; there is little doubt this has something to do with it.

Lucas and Moll used a model of how knowledge is acquired in society that you could describe as an accumulation of knowledge events that happen at some average rate — a kind of knowledge clock. In the real world, we have such a thing: DNA could be described as an accumulation of survival knowledge and the time between mutations is constant enough that geneticists can use the number of mutations as a clock to estimate when different species diverged relative to the observation time. In their model, it gets harder and harder to discover (or create) new technology (innovation), so it does make sense to talk about discovering nearly all possible technology. Lucas and Moll then look at what happens when you take *both* the observation time and the time between ticks of the knowledge clock to be infinity.

Now you can probably feel that this doesn't make a lick of sense. And sure enough Paul Romer jumped on it. But Romer's critique doesn't make a lick of sense either, for Romer proudly, in rigorous mathematical proposition form no less, expounded his critique by proving a theorem you might see in a real analysis course (a staple of math majors everywhere, and colloquially known as the "weed-out" course for math majors at the University of Texas) that the double limit fails to converge uniformly. That is to say you get different results depending on whether you take the clock time to infinity or the observation time to infinity first.

If there are never any mutations in DNA, then even if you observe the DNA in the infinite future, there still aren't any mutations. But if you observe in the infinite future, all the mutations have happened, no matter how slow they accrue. So you either have no mutations or all the mutations. After reading this, I probably looked a bit like Danny in Stanley Kubrick's movie *The Shining* in the scene where he encounters the twins on his big wheel.

Aside from not being something you encounter in the real world, one of the curious things about infinity is that it doesn't have any units. In the same way that two times infinity doesn't make sense, infinity seconds also doesn't make sense. This means you can't really take the clock time (with units of second between ticks) or the observation time (in units of seconds since the start of civilization, I guess) to infinity separately. This is because those numbers represent (a possible) real universe.

You can however, take the ratio of the two measures, which has units of seconds divided by seconds (which cancel, leaving no units) to infinity or zero. Or as a physicist might say: you can say the clock time is very short or very long compared to the observation time period. These are two different limits and lead to the two different results above. In a sense Lucas and Moll chose one of them — which is perfectly fine. Paul Romer's critique was that there are two limits, and you can't choose between them.

Ah, but you can! Again, it's because what you are studying represents a real universe. The limit Lucas and Moll use is the one where all the mutations have happened. The other limit is the one where mutations never happen. So you have two universes: one where things happen and one where nothing ever happens. Which one do you think is real? This could be considered an appeal to the so-called anthropic principle in physics — the universe has to appear a certain way because we exist in order to observe it.

Now I don't think this indicts every economist or means every physicist is superior. For example, the physicist Tom Murphy (who is a colleague of a close friend of mine) once made some comments about how economic growth cannot continue forever that effectively assumes the ratio of Gross Domestic Product (GDP) to annual energy consumption is constant. It's true that the eventual heat death of the universe puts a damper on things, but like Nicolas Georgescu-Roegen — who made a similar point using finite entropy production — this limit isn't particularly sensible. And we don't have far to look for an example where contribution to GDP doesn't depend strongly on energy consumption: the financial sector. Their entire service consists of charging lots of money to move bits around (and keeping a bit for themselves) which theoretically could cost a minuscule amount of energy (there is actually a number for this, and it's tiny). This isn't to say Murphy isn't smart or that growth can continue indefinitely, it's just that the issue isn't terribly relevant to our current situation.

I do think economics could benefit from physicists on how to apply math. These limits (as they are called in math) where for example the rate of DNA mutations is much faster or slower than the observation time period — the two time scales of the theory — form the basis of *scope conditions* or *regions of validity* of a theory or model. These rules define when we can and when we can't use a specific theory or model. We didn't throw out all of Newtonian physics when Einstein developed his theory of relativity. What happened was that we made explicit the scope of Newtonian physics — slow speeds compared to the speed of light, low gravitational field strengths, and a given level of precision. So we used Newtonian physics when we sent humans to the Moon, but use Einstein's theory of gravity to make GPS precise (there's an important correction due to clocks running slower for us on Earth, deeper in the gravitational field than the GPS satellites). We knew about some of these limitations through experiments, but Einstein's theories gave us ways to explicitly show them. You can in fact derive Newtonian physics from Einstein's theories by using approximations where the speed of light is really fast compared to the velocities encountered in the solar system. As yet, we don't have any scope conditions for Einstein's theory of gravity, but we think they fail when you get to really short distances because of quantum mechanics (the scale involved is called the Planck length). We don't know that for sure, but that's the general consensus.

Lucas and Moll's model only applies when innovation is fast compared to the time period you observe the economy — observing an economy for a long time. Similarly, there are macroeconomic models where it is assumed that the central bank reacts faster than the central government to a changing economy. However, economists tend to fail to explicitly point this out. Theories (and especially results) in economics are presented as if they are Einstein's theory of gravity — without scope conditions. However, every assumption in a model yields a scope condition. Assuming rational agents, as I will discuss later, is assuming you are close to an economic equilibrium. The shifts in supply and demand curves in introductory economics assume one or the other adapts faster. In another example I will discuss later, most economic theories assume a large number of people. Therefore those theories should not be assumed apply to small numbers of people. It is this thinking in terms of scale and scope that I'd hope economics could learn from physics.

Not all fields deal with numerical data, so math isn't always required. Not a single equation appears in Darwin's *Origin of Species*, for example. And while there exist many cases where economics studies unquantifiable behavior of humans, a large portion of the field is dedicated to understanding numerical quantities like prices, interest rates, and GDP growth. The primary purpose of mathematical theory is to provide equations that illustrate relationships between sets of numerical data. That what Galileo was doing when he was rolling balls down inclined planes (comparing distance rolled and time measured with water flowing), discovering distance was proportional to the square of the water volume (i.e. time). Math is helpful in describing systems only inasmuch as the math leads to useful relationships between numerical measurements and empirical data. Useful here doesn't mean 100% accurate. Relationships can be useful but only approximate. However it is only after filling in the variables in the equations do we get a sense of the scales involved and the scope of the theory.

Random people

Economist and Nobel laureate Gary Becker doesn't seem like a great starting place to undermine the edifice of neoclassical economics. He was part of the so-called Chicago School (named after the University of Chicago) with Milton Friedman. He led a conservative push to try to replace sociology with economics. He produced theoretical research that supported the idea that high levels of punishment combined low probability of being caught would reduce crime — which fed into lengthening prison sentences. Today, the United States has one of the largest populations behind bars in the world. The thing is he believed in rational economic agents so much that in his zeal to defend the idea he made rational economic agents unnecessary.

In 1962, Gary Becker published a paper titled "Irrational Behavior and Economic Theory". Becker's purpose was to immunize economics against attacks on the idealized rational agents typically assumed in models. After briefly sparking a debate between Becker and Israel Kirzner (that seemed to end abruptly), the paper appears to have been largely forgotten — or at least its main lesson has.

Becker's main argument was that ideal rationality

was not as critical to microeconomic theory because random agents can be used to reproduce some important theorems. Let me briefly give an overview of the argument, followed with a more detailed and concrete version. Consider the opportunity set (the set or space of available choices) and budget constraint (limited money constraining those choices) for two goods: pints of blueberries and pints of raspberries. An agent may select any point inside the budget constraint by purchasing some number of pints of blueberries and some number of pints of raspberries. In order to find which point the agents select, economists typically introduce a utility function for the agents (one type of berry may produce more utility than the other) and then solves for the maximum utility on the opportunity set. This produces a triangular set of opportunities that I'll illustrate after a couple of paragraphs. As the price changes for one berry (meaning more or less of that berry can be bought given the same budget constraint), the shape of the triangle changes, and the utility maximizing point on the opportunity set moves. The effect of these price changes selects a different point on the opportunity set, tracing out one of those demand curves you've likely seen in a supply and demand diagram.

Instead of the agents selecting a point through utility maximization, Becker assumed every point in the triangular opportunity set was equally likely —

that agents selected points in the opportunity set at random, fully exploring it. In this case, the average is at the "center of mass" of the triangular region inside the budget constraint. However, Becker showed that changing the price of one of the goods still produced a demand curve just like in the utility maximization case; he derived the economics of supply and demand from random behavior.

Since this is important to the rest of my critique, I'm going to give an explicit example of the argument Gary Becker makes in his paper. Let's say you have two choices for things to spend money on. They could be blueberries and raspberries (as above) or blueberries now and blueberries later (so-called "intertemporal" or "between times" consumption). Let's say you have a limited amount of money: $20. That's your budget constraint. If blueberries and raspberries are each $4 per pint, then you could buy 1 pint of blueberries and 4 pints of raspberries (for example). Let's represent the number of pints of blueberries as the first number in a pair and the number of pints of raspberries as the second number. That example would be (1, 4). What are all the possibilities?

(0, 5), (1, 4), (2, 3), (3, 2), (4, 1), (5, 0),
(0, 4), (1, 3), (2, 2), (3, 1), (4, 0),
(0, 3), (1, 2), (2, 1), (3, 0),
(0, 2), (1, 1), (2, 0),
(0, 1), (1, 0),
(0, 0)

This is the opportunity set (a physicist would say "state space"). On the first line, you spend all of your $20. On the second, you spend $16. On the third, you spend $12, and so on down to zero. Note this makes that triangle I mentioned above, and would also make a triangle if you represented it on an x-y axis graph (albeit not with exactly the same appearance as the triangle above, but that isn't important right now).

Assuming each opportunity is equally likely, the average is about (2, 2) meaning you buy 2 pints of blueberries, 2 pints of raspberries, and have $4 left over from your $20. The actual average is really more like (1.7, 1.7) and you have $6.67 left over (on average), but (2, 2) is good enough for us.

The assumption of each choice being equally likely is what Becker calls "irrational". If I'm presented with a choice, and you have no idea what I'll choose (because I'm "irrational"), then your best guess is taking each possibility as equally likely. However, this is also the starting point physicists take when looking at large collections of atoms. It is an assumption of *our own* ignorance — at the time when Ludwig Boltzmann first made it, ignorance that atoms even existed! I wouldn't refer to atoms as "irrational" — *random* maybe (or *mindless*), but not *irrational*.

Just because an economist doesn't know what I am going to do doesn't necessarily make me irrational; rather the economist might just be ignorant of the details of the situation. I might not buy any blueberries when I go to the store because I just discovered I'm allergic or I lost my job and need to save money for essentials. Or maybe I just don't feel like having blueberries. Humans are complicated, and even if they told you why they made a choice it doesn't mean that is the reason.

In the traditional "rational" approach to economics, you'd have to assign a preference to blueberries and raspberries. If you preferred blueberries a bit more to raspberries (and money), you could end up with exactly (3, 2), with no money left over. If you liked them both the same, you'd have (2.5, 2.5), again with no money left over. Those "solutions" would be exact and would rationally maximize your berry utility function because they yield the most berries in the proportions you liked.

What happens if the price of blueberries goes up to $8 per pint? Well, the opportunity set now looks like this:

(0, 5), (1, 3), (2, 1),
(0, 4), (1, 2), (2, 0),
(0, 3), (1, 1),
(0, 2), (1, 0),
(0, 1),
(0, 0)

You can see the shape of the opportunity set changed. The average is now about (1, 2) meaning you buy 1 pint of blueberries, 2 pints of raspberries and have $4 left over from your $20. The price of blueberries went up, and you (on average) bought fewer blueberries — that's the basic idea behind a demand curve. As the price of something goes up, you buy less of it.

Well, at least if the price of raspberries stayed the same and you still had $20 to spend. As the price of something goes up, you buy less of it *ceteris paribus* (using the Latin for "with other things the same" that economists frequently use). Also recognize that this is an average in Gary Becker's irrational agent model; you could go to the store and buy 5 pints of raspberries instead of the (2, 2) or (1, 2) solutions above. Individual observations do not have to conform to the most likely aggregate observation.

To me, this is a much more satisfying way to think about supply and demand. Instead of an optimization over an unobservable variable called utility yielding a single "solution", it recognizes that the quantity demanded, quantity supplied and the price can be noisy at the outset — that buying less after a price rise is not a foregone conclusion, just a tendency for a large number of observations and agents exploring the opportunity set. Optimization of an ostensibly good thing like utility in an objective function also makes you think in terms of trade-offs; if you are at an optimum deviating from it is less than optimal and encourages zero-sum thinking. Looking at the effects of supply and demand as simply the most likely observed state has no such consequences. Policies that cause the economy deviate from the optimum seem bad; policies that cause the economy to deviate from the most likely outcome may be good or bad.

Additionally, we now have two models that lead to qualitatively similar results. If you can get the exact same demand curves from utility maximizing agents and random ones, it calls into question the mental model behind supply and demand. It's also an example of how supply and demand or rational agents might be *emergent* concepts in the sense that no single agent experiences the forces of supply and demand or is as "rational" as *Homo economicus*, but a collection of multiple agents does and is. No single atom has a temperature or manifests diffusion, but a collection of multiple atoms does.

One of Economist John List's contributions to economics is expanding experimental economics started by economist Vernon Smith. Smith won a Nobel Prize in part for his effort to turn economics into a laboratory science. In List's 2004 paper "Testing Neoclassical Competitive Theory in Multilateral Decentralized Markets", he set up a field experiment. The goods up for exchange: several copies of a 1982 baseball card with a mustache drawn on them (I'm a bit surprised the player didn't already have one it being the 1980s). The venue: a sports card show. List gave the 14 buyers and 14 sellers participating in the experiment a "buyer's card" or a "seller's card" that told them how much they valued the baseball card.

One of the problems with giving people numerical values for the cards is that it effectively assumes the entire apparatus of the rational utility maximizing ("neoclassical") economic model. The buyer or seller's card tells the agent how much he or she values the baseball card. In real life, humans will change their valuation of something depending on conditions. A pint of blueberries at your house is worth, say, $5 before you put it in a smoothie, but worth almost zero before you head on a long vacation. If you give a person a number to follow, they become that number — a number that can be used to maximize — which is the underlying assumption of neoclassical economics. If we really had static numerical valuations of everything, then economics would be completely accurate and I wouldn't be writing this book.

The interesting thing is that giving people these numbers and telling them not to go over them creates a budget constraint. And in that case, everything that Gary Becker says about random agents follows.

I tested this hypothesis by writing a short computer program where buyers and sellers randomly encountered each other and buyers randomly offered prices to sellers that were below the number on the card. For example, if the buyer's card said $12, then on a chance meeting with a seller, the buyer would offer somewhere between $1 and $12 (say by rolling a 12-sided die familiar to *Dungeons & Dragons* players). Let's say the result was $6. If the randomly encountered seller had a reservation price of $3 on his or her seller's card (for example), then the sale would go through. If it was $10 on the seller's card, he or she wouldn't sell (the buyer didn't offer enough). The computer program would repeat this until no more sales could be made. The result was fairly close to the results List found in his field experiment.

So we find ourselves in a situation where we have two models — the neoclassical rational agent model and a random "irrational" agent model. Both models explain the field experiments. William of Occam would have said to select the one with the fewest assumptions (it's called "Occam's razor"), and were there no other data then obviously the irrational agent model wins. But experiments don't exist in a vacuum — other experiments exist.

Many experiments have shown that humans do not behave with economic rationality in one-human or two-human tests. One example is the so-called ultimatum game where real humans "irrationally" punish greedy players who divide a given payout unfairly, losing out on part of the payout themselves in order to send a message. So we know if the number of humans is small, the rational agent model is flawed. Maybe it still works for a larger number of humans — like the 28 in the field experiment? This isn't as silly as it might seem. If you've ever seen a political poll, they often quote a margin of error of about 3%. This isn't really the error of the poll result from the actual value. It's the error of the poll result assuming the poll was conducted under perfect conditions (without the biases of surveying land lines versus cell phones, for example) and as such a good first estimate of the error percentage is 100 divided by the square root of the number of people the poll questioned. The 100 is for converting to a percentage. That 3% means the poll was used a sample of about 1000 people: the square root of 1000 is about 32 and 100 divided by

32 is about 3, so 3%. For 3 people, that estimate of the error would be about 60%. For 28, that number is about 20%. In fact, the statistical error in the observed average prices in List's experiment are about 10 to 20% — about what you'd expect from having 28 people participating. (Also, the prices that appear in the market are about what you might expect from polling the participants — more on this later.)

So maybe the rational agent model is only good for a large number of people in a market? This is another example of a scope condition or a region of validity for a theory. This would mean that applying the rational agent theory to cases where there are only a few people is out of scope for the model. However the scope for the random agent model is essentially the same as the rational agent model, so that doesn't help us choose between them. However the random agent model does help explain something that would be kind of surprising were it not for the random agents.

Keith Chen (and his colleagues) set up an experiment where he trained capuchin monkeys to trade tokens for grapes and Jell-O. Once the monkeys got used to the idea, he tried to see what would happen if he made grapes more or less expensive in terms of tokens. As humans do, they bought fewer grapes and more Jell-O if grapes became more expensive. In a few papers, including one from 2005 titled "The Evolution of Our Preferences: Evidence from Capuchin Monkey Trading Behavior" written with Venkat Lakshminarayanan and Laurie Santos, Keith Chen presented the results as demonstrating rational choices.

Here, we have an example of economic framing of a result in evolutionary science even though there is no concrete proof that the specifics of that economic framing are happening. The results are completely consistent with Gary Becker's argument from properties of the opportunity set made up of the available number of tokens, and the prices of grapes and Jell-O. The monkeys may be acting with economic rationality, but they also might be "irrational" agents exploring the state space.

This should be troubling for other sciences. Most fields expect the results released in the textbooks of another field to be robust. Physicists don't put a specific theory of what dark matter is in a textbook because there is no consensus theoretical model of dark matter. It's made obvious that it's not founded on a robust theoretical result (it is a robust *experimental* result observed in galactic rotation speeds). However, the "rational agent" (I mean that in a generic sense) explanation of supply and demand is used in economics textbooks, not Gary Becker's "irrational agents".

To be fair, Chen found that capuchins also seemed to display similar behavioral deviations from rational behavior (like loss aversion, where one of two equivalent bets are less likely to be undertaken if that one is framed as a loss). However, experiments where traditional microeconomics appears to arise spontaneously should not be very surprising if considered as properties of the opportunity set, not the agents. From Vernon Smith's experiments using human students at the University of Arizona to Keith Chen's experiments using capuchin monkeys at Yale, most agents capable of exploring the opportunity set (state space) will manifest some microeconomic behavior.

* * *

These two plausible yet different models for the basic economic force of supply and demand have additional ramifications for prediction markets. In addition to the "information discovery" mechanism, prediction markets are supposed to have the additional advantage of rewarding good predictions and punishing bad predictions. You could call it an "error correction" mechanism. If you make bad predictions ("Mitt Romney will win the 2012 Presidential election"), you will lose money. If you make good predictions, you will make money.

If your predictions represented the actual movement of supply and demand curves (changes in Becker's opportunity set), then this would in fact be true. As long as the probability of finding agents remains roughly uniform across the opportunity set, changes in price reflect actual changes in supply and demand. However, what if everyone panicked (or there was some new diet fad or other forms of so-called groupthink) and decided to stock up on raspberries instead of blueberries? Or decided to consume blueberries in the future as opposed to the present? What if everyone became correlated?

In that case, the price would fail to represent movements of the supply and demand curves (changes in the opportunity set). There are no changes in the opportunity set itself, just changes in how the agents explore it. It is a market failure. However, predictions (options contracts) would still be rewarded (or punished) even if they represent no change in the underlying opportunity set. What was previously a one-way valve letting good information in and sending bad information out would become a two-way valve letting bad information in — people who just got lucky.

Now how do economists determine if prediction markets are working? Well, one metric is to look at the price versus the eventual payoff. If the market is "efficient", then this should show a 1-to-1 relationship (a high price for a high payoff and a low price for a low payoff). This method was employed by economists Bo Cowgill and Eric

Zitzewitz in their 2015 paper "Corporate Prediction Markets: Evidence from Google, Ford, and Firm X". As a side note, after a bit of digging on the Internet I found some evidence in an earlier version of the paper that "Firm X" was actually Koch Industries, the CEOs of which are notable conservative free market advocates. The prediction markets were set up by the companies to forecast, for example, how many vehicles would be sold (at Ford). They found that the prediction markets obeyed this 1-to-1 relationship and concluded the markets were working.

Does this mean the markets were aggregating diffused knowledge to find conclusions? It could be, but it could also be aggregating Becker's irrational agents. Let's take the different berries to instead be different time periods. Let's say one is the present (the present price) and one is the eventual future (payoff).

The center of mass of that triangle, if we say both legs (as opposed to the hypotenuse) are the same length (as Cowgill and Zitzewitz do by normalizing their prices), is going to give us a 1-to-1 relationship between the price and the payoff. The high price, low payoff and low price, high payoff results are way in the corners of the triangle. Rarely will all the agents congregate in those corners if they are fully exploring the opportunity set. The bulk of states in this intertemporal opportunity set will have prices and payoffs proportional to each other — and after normalization, produce a straight line. Irrational agents can produce the exact same 1-to-1 relationship that economists saw as a demonstration that the prediction markets were working as described by rational agents. If the only metric you have for the efficacy of prediction markets is such that humans are no different than capuchin monkeys wandering around the same opportunity set, how much do you trust that the prediction market is working?

* * *

Gary Becker's irrational agents lets us use two different vantage points from which to view economics. There's one that relies on human decision-making and one that doesn't. And it is our human bias towards our own agency that chooses one over the other.

Imagine if physics had two different explanations of electricity — one that used mindless particles and one that used little living homunculi carrying buckets of "electrical fluid". Usually in science, if you have two explanations, one works better than the other but let's say both theories are equally good at explaining experimental data. Our bias (in today's world) would be toward the theory with the particles — Occam's razor. We don't go for explanations that involve little creatures as much as mechanistic ones in physics. However, if the data is explained by both theories, we really must rely on some external principle in order to distinguish them. Occam's razor (that the simplest explanation is best) is one such principle, and in this electricity example it would lead to choosing mindless particles.

Yet it doesn't yield the baseline result when confronted with "random" agents versus rational agents — both explaining the data as well as the other. In that case, I think the bias in economic theory is toward our own human agency.

Another dimension

I'm going to expand on Gary Becker's argument. Let's say you have $20 in your pocket to spend on bulk berries at the store. In the first scenario, they only have blueberries. In that case you could spend all $20 on blueberries, or you could spend $5 on blueberries and hold onto the remaining $15. If I had to guess how much you'd spend given that the only thing I knew about you was that you had $20, my best guess would be to say you'd spend $10 and hold onto $10. These possibilities are called an opportunity set in economics. A physicist would call it a state space.

Now let's play this same game with three kinds of berries: blueberries, blackberries, and raspberries. You could spend $1 on blueberries, $1 on blackberries, $1 on raspberries, and hold onto $17. You could spend $20 on blueberries and nothing on raspberries. You could spend $6 on each and hold onto $2. In this scenario, my best guess would be that you'd spend about $5 on blueberries, $5 on blackberries, $5 on raspberries, and hold onto $5.

What about for nine kinds of berries? Blueberries, blackberries, raspberries, huckleberries, salmonberries, lingonberries, strawberries, boysenberries and gooseberries. In this scenario, my best guess would be $2 on each and that you'd hold onto $2.

Now this game doesn't work if there's an outbreak of some fad (blueberries as a "superfood"). My guess for how much kale someone walking into Whole Foods Market would buy has increased several-fold over the last few years. If we as humans all do the same things — if we are correlated — this trick doesn't work. This is important to remember for later.

However, notice as we add different kinds of berries, the total amount I'd guess you'd hold onto becomes less and less? For one type of berry, you hold onto $10. For three types, you hold onto $5. For nine types, you hold onto $2. If there were huge number of types of berries, you'd likely spend all your money. An economist would say you saturate your budget constraint.

The different kinds of berries give us the dimension of the opportunity set we're examining: 1, 3 or 9. Those dimensions in economics could represent different kinds of goods and services (i.e. berries, kale or Pilates classes), or different time periods. For example, you have a monthly budget for blueberries of $20 and you go to the store every week or so spending $3 one day, $2 another and $10 the last trip to the store during the month, taking a week off. That's four time periods or four dimensions.

In his paper, Gary Becker made saturating a budget constraint an assumption because he only looked at two goods or time periods. But you don't have to make this assumption if you just look at a large number of time periods or have a large number of different choices of goods. Basically, if the dimension of the opportunity set is large — and people aren't correlated — you saturate your budget constraint. In more ordinary language, if the number of choices you have is large and there aren't fads leading to any of the specific choices, you'll spend all your money. This is the result of a general property that a typical high dimensional shape has: most of its volume is near its surface.

An interesting consequence when you think of the different dimensions as buying blueberries in different time periods is *consumption smoothing*: the average location is not only near the (intertemporal) budget constraint hyperplane (the surface of the opportunity set hypervolume where "hyper" just means "in a higher dimension"), but in the middle of that hyperplane if there is nothing special about any of the time periods. On average, each period has the same level of blueberry consumption assuming each period is roughly the same. Normally, this is enforced as an assumption about agents' rationality in economic models. Milton

Friedman called it the "Permanent Income Hypothesis" where agents make consumption decisions based on their expected future income, not just this week's paycheck. In his 1978 paper "Stochastic Implications of the Life Cycle-Permanent Income Hypothesis", Robert Hall showed that consumption smoothing was a consequence of rational utility maximizing behavior of the agents. In our case however, it is derived from the dimension and symmetry of the opportunity set.

Like before, we have two models that produce the same result. Optimizing rational agents and random agents lead to the same response to price changes, regardless of the number of choices (dimensions). Both lead to saturating the budget constraint if there are a lot of choices or time periods. Now, both lead to consumption smoothing if there are a lot of time periods.

In physics, there are plenty of examples where two very different models produce the same results. In the late 90s, it was discovered that a four-dimensional particle theory could produce the same results as a five-dimensional gravitational theory (both part of a ten-dimensional string theory). From the perspective of the four-dimensional particle theory, the additional dimension and the gravitational theory *emerge* in a particular limit of the theory. Some things are easier to calculate using one theory; some things are easier using the other.

Like the emergent dimension in physics, one way we can think about our two models producing the same results is that the rational agent is *emergent* in the random agent model. This would resolve a major issue in economics: many macroeconomic models assume rational agents even though behavioral economics frequently finds evidence against them in experiments with one or a few people. Emergent rational agents would solve this problem by saying the rational agent model is out of scope for the behavior of one person. *H. economicus* disperses into thousands of "irrational" *H. sapiens* as we zoom in — much like the photos in newspapers or Pointillist paintings become a jumble of different colored dots when viewed up close (or like the sovereign on the frontispiece of Thomas Hobbes' *Leviathan* made up of multitudes of people).

If this is the case, we'd really have to be careful about applying lessons of economics derived from *H. economicus* to *H. sapiens*. The former might smooth consumption, but the latter will have no such restriction. We'd also have to be careful about when we apply *H. economicus*. If the number of choices, time periods, or agents aren't very big, then we can't take the shortcut of starting with rational agents.

However, it gets more interesting. In a 2016 paper

titled "How Does Unemployment Affect Consumer Spending?" by Peter Ganong and Pascal Noel, people do not appear to smooth consumption when they experience shocks to income. This is problematic for the Permanent Income Hypothesis and rational agents, but the consumption smoothing derived from random agents shouldn't be expected to hold when there are shocks. When unemployment insurance benefits expire, agents will probably make correlated decisions to cut back on spending — they're no longer behaving randomly (or rather, with such complexity it looks random).

There is one really big lesson. One view of a recession is that everyone holds back on their spending — Keynes' paradox of thrift. This shouldn't happen for rational agents — even emergent ones. That means one of our assumptions necessary for rational agents to emerge from random agents must not be valid. But which one? One possible answer is the assumption that our random agents fully explore the opportunity set. Everyone cutting back on spending means the agents aren't fully exploring the opportunity set. In physics, if the state space isn't fully explored, entropy isn't maximized and we say the system is not in equilibrium. If we carry this analogy over to economics, then we could say that just like how *H. economicus* falls apart when we zoom in on one individual, *H. economicus* falls apart we move away from economic equilibrium. Is this why many macroeconomic models failed during the Great Recession?

Another conclusion that comes to the forefront derives from the fact that a higher dimensional state space is directly related to increased diversity in the system. In an analogy I borrowed from Diane Coyle's 2014 book *GDP: A Brief but Affectionate History*, a spoon, a knife, and a fork is more valuable than three spoons. Cesar Hidalgo makes a similar point in his book *Why Information Grows: The Evolution of Order, from Atoms to Economies* using a measure of economic complexity or diversity, showing it is proportional to GDP *per capita*. It could be that in the same way that maximizing biodiversity maximizes the average fitness of an ecosystem, maximizing economic choices — choices that aren't closed off due to lack of money — maximizes overall prosperity.

Going forward, we should ask how many of the failures of the traditional rational agent approach we can understand with the emergent rational agent. However we should also ask exactly how much of the traditional rational agent approach to economics can be understood with the emergent rational agent. Can random agents produce all of the results understood with optimizing rational agents — especially the non-trivial ones?

Advantage: E. coli

> *The anecdote is famous. A mathematician, Stan Ulam, once challenged [economist] Paul Samuelson to name one proposition in the social sciences that is both true and non-trivial. His reply was: "Ricardo's theory of comparative advantage".... Truth, however, in Samuelson's reply refers to the fact that [economist David] Ricardo's theory of comparative advantage is mathematically correct, not that it is empirically valid.*

That's the opening paragraph of Arnaud Costinot and Dave Donaldson's 2012 paper "Ricardo's Theory of Comparative Advantage: Old Idea, New Evidence". The non-trivial aspect of Ricardo's theory is that even countries that are more efficient at producing everything will still engage in trade as it is advantageous for both countries to do so. The traditional explanation from Ricardo tells us that it is not the absolute efficiency, but rather the relative efficiency that is dictating this result. Even if the United States is less efficient at producing blueberries than Canada, it could still find itself exporting blueberries to Canada because the United States is marginally more efficient at producing blueberries than it is raspberries. This trade is mutually beneficial to both countries — it's positive-sum, not zero-sum.

That's where the idea gets its name: it's not absolute advantage (absolute efficiency), but comparative advantage (relative efficiency). But is it the rigorous look at the numbers implied by Ricardo that determines the amount of blueberry trade between the US and Canada? Actually Costinot and Donaldson find that Ricardo's theory doesn't exactly match the data:

> *While the slope coefficient falls short of its theoretical value (one), it remains positive and statistically significant.*

You could say there's only a tendency towards the positive-sum gains from trade the theoretical comparative advantage argument, with the real world falling short.

However, is this the only way to obtain this result? If you combine the opportunity sets of two nations, it is highly unlikely that the equilibrium will be the same as for the two nations separately unless the opportunity sets are identical. In fact, you generally increase the dimension and volume of the consumption opportunity set — adding regions of the opportunity set inaccessible to each nation alone — leading to more overall consumption and a larger economy. If you allow trade, industries on either side of the US-Canada border could wander into this new state with more blueberries overall. And since the state described by Ricardo is possible — and involves more overall consumption of blueberries — the final result would likely be somewhere between the full Ricardo solution and the no-trade solution.

This is basically what Costinot and Donaldson find. It is therefore not just possible but advantageous to describe comparative advantage a property of the opportunity set, not the agents. Agents just randomly wander into available states.

Agents randomly wandering into available states is also a great description of biological evolution. And it thus seems odd that biologists would be interested in an explanation of metabolic exchange resting on a theoretical framework that takes into account the desires (utility) of agents. It has happened, though. In "An Economic Framework of Microbial Trade", a 2015 paper by economist Joshua Tasoff and biologists Michael Mee and Harris Wang, the authors use comparative advantage to theoretically describe a colony of *E. coli* (a species of bacteria commonly used in research) — it's a great paper and an interesting result.

In that paper, the scientists thankfully abandon the explanation in terms of utility, substituting growth as the objective function. But it still means that bacteria are cooperating (mutualism) in order to collectively maximize growth. It makes far more sense from the perspective of biology and its well-established evolutionary framework if the metabolic exchange arose by evolutionary trial-and-error from simply exploring the metabolic opportunity set through random mutations.

Like the case of the capuchin monkeys, we see that economists have done a disservice to other scientific fields that take their results at face value. It is true that comparative advantage is what economics as a field believes is correct and teaches it as the rational outcome of weighing opportunity costs. But that is not the only way to obtain this result, and biologists would likely be keener on the random exploration of opportunities derived from Gary Becker's approach with its stronger similarities to mindless evolutionary processes.

And this brings up a new issue that we didn't have with monkeys. Capuchin monkeys arguably have nascent versions of the mental faculties humans possess. However, if the economic framework applies to bacteria what exactly is the human brain bringing to the table? The normal "rational utility maximizing" Operating System (rum-OS) is typically assumed to run on a processor called a "brain". In capuchin monkeys we are seeing rum-OS running on a much less capable processor. With *E. coli* we seem to be seeing the same output of the rum-OS running on a single transistor. That is to say maybe the software behind the rum-OS isn't really that complicated and doesn't call the various functions of a brain like consciousness. In the old x86 chips you could add a math co-processor. If a program ran as fast with or without the math co-processor, it probably wasn't using it. In the same way, the rum-OS probably isn't using much of the brain that couldn't be accomplished with a single neuron or even inside a single cell. Could it be our capacity to plan for the future? That's the subject of the next chapter.

Great Expectations

In economics, agents have beliefs about the future called expectations. Expectations are critically important to all economics — both that part of economics where economists talk about "the economy" as if it's one big system, and the individual firms, households, and people. Expectations are about inflation, Gross Domestic Product (GDP) growth, your future consumption of blueberries, or any number of other fluctuating variables. Central banks like the United States' Federal Reserve Bank ("the Fed") or the Bank of England can attempt to set inflation expectations for their respective countries. The can be "anchored" or "unanchored" (particularly in regard to inflation) meaning people's expectations are hard to change or hard to stop from changing, respectively.

Economists tend to put them in their equations by putting capital E's on or around the symbols for future inflation (or prices). Sometimes they are lowercase e's. What this means is that the equations use some model for expectations, the most common being "rational" (also known as "model-consistent") expectations.

Rational expectations means that if future inflation as determined by the model is the center of a dart board, then the people in the model mess up their dart forecasting inflation equally in all directions. We don't guess too high or too low on average. Sounds reasonable on the surface — at least for a first guess. However, the first time I saw this I laughed in the way only a physicist can find an equation funny.

Why is it funny? Because rational expectations means sticking that E on or around the symbol for future inflation makes the model depend on the actual value of future inflation in the model — the center of that dart board — so that in the model the present now depends on things that happen in the future. Let me illustrate the ramifications.

Scott Sumner, a Bentley University economics professor, wrote a blog post titled "How the interest rate increase of 2015 caused the Great Recession" — *in March of 2014*. He continues:

> *At first glance my hypothesis seems absurd for many reasons, primarily because effect is not suppose[d] to precede cause. So let me change the wording slightly, and suggest that expectations of this 2015 rate increase caused the Great Recession [in 2008]. Still seems like a long shot, but it's actually far more plausible than you imagine (and indeed is consistent with mainstream*

macro[economic] theory.)

The thing is that any model of inflation expectations that depends on the actual value of future inflation — of which rational expectations is but one version — will have this causality issue. The *E*'s move information about future inflation from the future into the present.

This is not quite as silly as it seems on its face. If company ABC announces on Monday it will buy company XYZ on the stock exchange for $20.00 per share on Friday, the stock price of company XYZ will rapidly rise from say $10.66 towards $19.77 (or some other value less than $20.00 to account for the fact that it costs money to trade stocks). In that case, the future price clearly had an impact on the present price.

But the Fed isn't ever promising to buy everything in the economy at a given consumer price index value (CPI, or price level). The Fed does have some control over the value of a dollar, so in a sense what they are doing in order to hit that inflation target (as it is called) is changing the value of the dollar such that the effect is the same as if they had bought everything in the economy at a given price level. This is not exactly right as the Fed doesn't think about the price level so much as the inflation rate (and other things like unemployment), but it is good enough for our purposes.

So now we need to know: Can (or will) the Fed change the value of a dollar? Is the Fed "credible" (the term of art)? In that stock example, if people thought it was only a 50-50 chance that company ABC would go through with that deal, the stock price might only rise to $15.00 — halfway between $10 and $20. The reasons could range from few investors believing company ABC has enough money or credit to buy the stock to some investors believing that the government won't approve the merger.

There are two reactions in economics to these attempts at mind-reading. One is to say: Of course it's important, but there's no way you'll pin it down with a mathematical model — you have to look to markets. The other is to say: Of course it's important, and we can pin it down with a model because people are mostly rational. In both cases the tendency is towards the importance of expectations.

Now expectations come from the agents (the microeconomics) in the model of the overall economy (the macroeconomics). Properties like rational expectations are a piece of so-called "microfoundations" — the microeconomic foundations of the macroeconomic model. The conventional narrative is that the introduction of rational expectations and microfoundations was a big revolution in economics in the 1970s. Up until that time, there was the view that the Phillips curve — a direct relationship between employment and inflation — was a macroeconomic property. If the central bank increased inflation, unemployment would go down.

Continuing the conventional narrative, the 1970s contained a period of high unemployment and high inflation (called "stagflation") that supposedly couldn't happen in the Phillips curve model. The solution, said people like economist Robert Lucas, was that people expected inflation (rationally); the Phillips curve broke down because it wasn't based on microfoundations including agents' expectations.

Oxford economist James Forder has done some historical research to show this isn't really what happened — there was never any claim that something like stagflation couldn't happen. Probably because of political changes at the time — in the US, government spending was being criticized, Ronald Reagan was just around the corner, and deregulation was already underway — the false narrative stuck. Sometimes what really happened in history isn't as big an influence as what people think happened. In the minds of economists, the Lucas critique (as it is called today) was devastating to macroeconomics built around Keynes' *General Theory* that had held sway in the halls of power.

Forward-looking expectations that depend on the actual future value of variables still dominate macroeconomics today. They may not be the simplistic rational expectations (the expected value is the future value plus a random error), but include limitations that go by names of bounded rationality, adaptive expectations, subjective expectations and belief revisions. From big names like Nobel laureate Paul Krugman (expectations explain the liquidity trap), Michael Woodford and Fed chairs Janet Yellen and Ben Bernanke to upstarts like Scott Sumner, macroeconomists include models of expectations that give non-zero weight to the actual future value of variables.

As we have seen, random people can explain the microeconomic world. Expectations are included because we want to make connection with the microeconomic world. Can we combine these disparate ideas in a sensible way? I don't think so. Now that I have fairly set up the plausibility and ubiquity of models depending on forward-looking expectations that depend on the actual future value of the expected variable, let me take them down.

Arbitrarily moving information from the future (the actual future value of inflation) into the present (making the current values of economic variables depend on future inflation) is problematic. To tell you why involves a bit of math, but it's math you can explain with dice.

If you roll one six sided die, assuming it's fair, each side should come up equally often. If you roll a pair of dice, as anyone who has shot craps or played *Monopoly* knows, there is a certain probability of each number between two and twelve coming up. Sevens come up a bunch because there are more ways to make seven from two dice than any other number (two plus five, three plus four, one plus six). There's only one way to get two (one plus one) and only one way to get twelve (six plus six).

As you roll more and more dice (as many a *Dungeons & Dragons* player such as myself has done), you will get closer and closer to the famous "bell curve" for the probabilities of the number you get when you add them together. The technical name is a "normal" (colloquially because it happens a lot, but may well have derived from its synonym "orthogonal") or Gaussian distribution (after the prolific mathematician Carl Friedrich Gauss, who actually didn't discover it). The probability of rolling all ones on ten dice (for a total of 10) less than 1 in a million. The probability hits its peak for rolling a 35 at just under 8%.

Speaking of *Dungeons & Dragons*, you'd get a bell curve if you used the 20-sided or 4-sided dice you use in the game as well. That's because of a mathematical theorem called the central limit theorem. The bell curve is a kind of universal distribution that you get as a result of adding up random "rolls" (random variables) from all kinds of distributions. That's what I meant by the "normal" distribution happening a lot.

In fact, you'd get the same normal distribution from any randomizing device (like rolling dice, or flipping coins) that has the same spread and average value. Twenty-sided dice would lead to a distribution with a wider spread and different average value than six-sided dice, but it is possible for a different distribution to give you the same normal distribution as a bunch of rolls six sided dice. One example would include adding up normal distributions!

The flip side of this universality is that information about how you got that normal distribution is lost. From a given normal distribution, you cannot work out the distribution you started with. If I told you the number of rolls and that it was fair die, you could probably estimate the number of sides it had. But without that extra information, you can't. That extra information is the information that was lost.

This is why it makes sense to project inflation out into the future given present information (some of the details of the present information will be lost due to the central limit theorem). However, this is also why it makes no sense for that value future inflation to have an influence on the present through expectations. You'd have to be able to undo the central limit theorem!

It should be noted that this is quite different from several different paths of the price level being consistent with some future price level target (or the potential indeterminacy involved with using interest rates to achieve an inflation target). It is the informational impossibility for a group of economic agents to create a specific distribution of price changes in the present that leads to a particular future distribution of the price level. Something has to tell people the distribution they should have.

There are two ways to solve this. One way is to say humans don't really have a say in it. The present distribution is a normal distribution, or some other non-informative distribution (dice rolls!), and humans are like a gas of atoms with little to no control over the process. The second way is to notice that this argument only applies if you use expectations models like rational expectations that use the actual value of future inflation as the expected value.

If the future value of inflation is just made up from information known at the present time, then there is no information being moved from the future to the present and no information problem. These kinds of models exist and range from simple "martingales" (one of prettier names in math where the last value is used as an estimate for the future value — for example, forecasting the weather tomorrow by saying it will be same as the weather today) to linear extrapolation to complex statistical models (autoregressive processes) that use several past values to estimate future ones.

That information problem makes those E's economists use what a physicist might technically call the inverse of a non-invertible operator (it's the inverse of a Koopman operator in dynamical systems). The forward direction takes multiple probability distributions to a single normal distribution. The reverse direction can't take us from that one normal distribution and find the (infinitely) many probability distributions that lead can lead to it. Such non-invertible operators are said to lose information — which makes sense as going into the future should get fuzzier and fuzzier the further we go. And it should make sense that we shouldn't be able to extract a crisp present from that fuzzy future.

* * *

If this technical issue with propagating information from the future into the present isn't enough for you, let me add a second problem. Forward-looking rational expectations models can allow a model to explain anything. Let's say we have a blueberry farmer. The farmer is credible such that if he says he'll produce 1000 pounds of blueberries in the spring, everyone believes him. Say the price of blueberries is expected to be $5 per pint because of the farmer's output. Everyone is working with the same mental model where if he grows more, the price goes down. If he grows less, the price goes up.

Let's say some blueberry buyers go out to the farm and notice that there's going to be way more than 1000 pounds of blueberries — more like 5000 pounds. They still believe the farmer wants to keep the price at $5 (because they think the farmer has hinted at it). The buyers invent stories where they expect the farmer will plow under the extra 4000 pounds of blueberries at the slightest drop in the price. Eventually, the full 5000 pounds of blueberries goes on the market. The price is still $5 because now the buyers expect that if the price goes up, the farmer will recall the extra 4000 pounds of blueberries.

In this parable, expectations overcame the underlying simple model of supply changes with roughly constant demand. The farmer was able to sell 5000 pounds of blueberries at $5, instead of the price dropping. The actual concrete actions by the farmer were insufficient to dislodge the expectations. As soon as you recognize expectations can be more powerful than the mechanisms in the model (the simple supply model), expectations can do anything.

This may seem like an abstract example, but it is actually the story of Japan since the early 2000s — just change out blueberries with Yen, the farmer with the Bank of Japan, and the buyers with the Japanese economy. Since around the year 2000, the amount of Yen available to the economy has gone up by about 5 times if you measure using currency and central bank reserves (called the monetary base, or you could say it about doubled if you just use printed currency). However, inflation has been about zero (the value of the Yen hasn't changed). Normal supply and demand for money would predict a fall in the value of a Yen with the drastically increased supply — inflation.

One theory that explains this strange occurrence is called a "liquidity trap", and it has been popularized by Nobel laureate and economist Paul Krugman. Originally proposed by Keynes, it's basically that expectations argument with the blueberries. In the modern version, the Bank of Japan has so much credibility in controlling inflation everyone thinks that were inflation to go up even a little bit the Bank of Japan would immediately start withdrawing up to 80% of the monetary base. As Krugman says, the bank can't credibly promise to be irresponsible (i.e. let inflation go above 1%). Even though the bank has stated it wants higher inflation, the Bank of Japan can't credibly create expectations of higher inflation. In that case, monetary policy becomes ineffective (and fiscal policy takes on a bigger role).

Another explanation (from a minority of economists) is that despite various statements from the Bank of Japan that it would like higher inflation, it actually doesn't want higher inflation. It's not that it's not credible, it's duplicitous. This lets this other economic model hold onto effective monetary policy. However, economists would have to use empirical inflation (or other measures of the value of Yen such as the exchange rate) as the economic model. That could of course explain *any* outcome. If inflation was 3%, then that means the Bank of Japan really wants 3% inflation. If inflation was 19%, then that means the Bank of Japan really wanted 19% inflation.

Now either of these could be what is really happening. The second view has the added benefit of being consistent with any possible set of inflation data. But maybe we should question the original model? The idea that "printing money" (or devaluing it relative to something shiny) leads to inflation is mostly based on situations where inflation is high. In that case, expectations don't seem to matter. Many studies have shown that in the case of high inflation, inflation is directly related to monetary base growth. It even appears in David Romer's graduate textbook *Advanced Macroeconomics* (4th ed. 2011). The expectations model actually supplants the original quantity of money picture.

It's not the amount of money printed, but the amount expected to be printed. That the quantity actually printed and the quantity expected to be printed match becomes more of a coincidence than a robust model success.

However, as the evidence comes from high inflation cases, maybe the simple supply model of money should be restricted in scope to high inflation cases. In fact, from the data we can give a specific number for that scope condition: monetary base growth and inflation of about 10% per year (defining a scale of 0.1/year, or its inverse equal to 10 years). Above that, inflation and base growth are tightly linked. Below that, something else is going on. In that view, the low inflation environments the US, EU and Japan find themselves in today don't satisfy the scope conditions of the theory. Instead of changing the theory to depend entirely on expectations for all values of inflation, we can have a new theory for low inflation.

There are a few possible choices. First, maybe expectations become more important at low inflation. This is essentially saying one of the theories above apply when inflation is low. Second, maybe the supply model of money breaks down at low inflation rates. In that case modifying it with expectations would be incorrect — we need a new theory. Third, maybe the simple supply theory is wrong altogether and it's just an approximation (valid at high inflation) to what is really happening.

The real problem is that expectations not only undo the success of the simple supply model of money, but allow anything to happen. This is not the kind of freedom that helps understanding. Much like how magical thinking can explain any natural observation and so explain nothing (to paraphrase Karl Popper), attributing economic outcomes to Green Lantern-like expectations also explains nothing. A restrictive theoretical framework is a necessary foundation of scientific inquiry. In physics, this came about with Isaac Newton. He wrote down a few rules that defined a theoretical framework that is alive and well today. Economics once had a framework with supply and demand, but the addition of expectations rendered any meaningful restriction that framework provided moot.

Rigid like elastic

Because more young adults are becoming unemployed on account of they can't find work. Basically, the problem is this: if you haven't got a job, then you're outta work! And that means only one thing – unemployment!

The Young Ones (1982) "Demolition"

One very important, but fairly technical idea in economics goes by the name of "nominal rigidity". More colloquially, it is called sticky prices. Sticky prices means prices don't respond to changing conditions as fast as economists assumed prices move in the first place. Now you may say: Why did economists assume prices moved quickly in the first place? That is a good question. It seems a bit like assuming snails are fast and then being puzzled that they are slow and saying they have "velocity rigidity". There are actually a surprising number of "puzzles" like that in economics.

Originally, economists thought prices would adjust to conditions relatively quickly. If there is a glut of blueberries, farmers have a financial incentive to lower their prices to sell them off before they go bad. Blueberry pickers should accept lower wages rather than lose their jobs and get nothing.

Along came the Great Depression, and economists saw a situation that could be described as gluts of blueberries and lots of unemployed pickers. Why didn't someone just take a lower paying job? Why didn't the farmers lower the price for their blueberries to sell them off? One solution to this (besides the laughable "great vacation" explanation where blueberry pickers prefer to be unemployed) was sticky prices.

If wages were sticky for example, then a shock to the economy would cause unemployment instead of having everyone employed at lower wages. There are lots of explanations for why this might be true ranging from employers thinking wage cuts lower morale (but they still cut hours in those situations) to unions refusing to agree to lower wages to people preferring no job to the same job at a lower wage (lest that new lower wage become a new anchor for their future employment) to workers being unable to coordinate wage cuts (instead taking their chances they won't be the ones being let go).

Those may be great explanations of wage stickiness and unemployment, but blueberries don't have preferences, morale, or unions. And if there is a general glut — too much of everything — then the price of everything should come down. Economists invented reasons for prices not to fall. One example is so-called menu costs: it costs money to change the price of a blueberry shake on your menu, so people hold back in doing it. If you've ever been to a restaurant where the prices are crossed out with a pen and written over or a "6" is turned into an "8", you can understand how strange of an assumption that is to make.

And sticky prices aren't just important when the shock hits. According to modern economics, the only reason we listen to statements from Federal Reserve Chair Janet Yellen is because of sticky prices. If prices are sticky, changes in the amount of money — monetary policy — can boost the economy or cause a recession. If prices weren't sticky, lowering interest rates and increasing the amount of money in the economy would head to a higher price for blueberries as fast as a fast snail. The current consensus macroeconomic stabilization policy framework depends on the existence of sticky prices.

What happens if you look at price data, though? It turns out sticky prices are not observed. In a 2008 paper ("Reference Prices and Nominal Rigidities"), Martin Eichenbaum, Nir Jaimovich and Sergio Rebelo say "our evidence is inconsistent with the three most widely used pricing models in macroeconomics." But even in that paper there is an attempt to rationalize that sticky prices still exist:

they claim that "reference prices" are sticky but "sale prices" aren't. Logically, this doesn't seem to be much different from saying they found out prices have a sticky component and a flexible component and the sticky component is still sticky.

The thing is even if you have a reference price and a 20% off sale price, and you trigger on and off the sale price every couple of weeks, you can still get an effective average price anywhere between the reference price and 20% off the reference price. The principle is similar to the game *Flappy Bird* where you press a button, click a mouse, or tap your touchscreen to "flap". With a series of on/off flaps (analogous to turning on and off sale prices), you can achieve almost any effective altitude for your bird (analogous to the effective price). Since people buy things at different times, the effective price seen by "the market" can look like a perfectly flexible market price.

The other problem is that the macroeconomic stabilization policies that depend on sticky prices seem to have the desired effect. In aggregate prices do seem to be sticky.

Let's turn to something that isn't rigid: elastic. What gives elastic polymers their elasticity? Polymers are long chains of atoms that tend to be flexible at room temperature. On their own, you tend to find them balled up like the tangle of extension cords everyone has at home. If you grab onto either end of a polymer molecule (you can do this using optical tweezers) and pull it straight, you can measure the resistance to your effort. And if you let go, the polymer will ball up again. What is this force? Well, as long as you don't pull the polymer completely straight to the point where you start pulling against the atomic bonds, there is no "real" force. It's a "fake" force called an entropic force (after thermodynamic entropy). You are literally pulling against probability. If it weren't for the fact that there are so many atoms in the chain, there wouldn't be any force to pull against. But because the chain is long, it is very unlikely for it to be in its straight state. Becoming straight means the chain loses its entropy, which costs energy, hence the force exerted by you acting over the distance that you stretch it.

One of the more familiar entropic forces is diffusion: if you drop cream in your coffee, it will form swirls and eventually blend completely. There is no real force acting on individual microscopic cream droplets spreading the cream around, it just becomes overwhelmingly likely that the cream is dispersed throughout the coffee over time.

What does this have to do with economics? Well, sticky prices look exactly like the elastic polymer's resistance to change. When you look at the system closely (at individual prices or at individual atoms) there is no resistance (stickiness or elasticity). But when you look at the system as a whole, it just becomes overwhelmingly unlikely that a bunch of prices will move in a particular direction or the polymer will unfurl itself.

If that is true, looking for empirical evidence of sticky prices at the individual good level or for an agent-level explanation of sticky wages is misguided. There is no useful agent-level explanation in the same way there is no useful atom-level explanation of elasticity or diffusion. Remember the microfoundations we discussed earlier? The existence of entropic forces in economics — forces that arise simply because there is a large number of things in an economy — would mean your job of building a model would be done as soon as you identified that there are a large number of things in your economic model. High unemployment might persist because it is just highly improbable that everyone without a job will find one all at once.

You might be asking yourself: If there is resistance to moving everyone into job state, there is presumably resistance to moving everyone out of a job state, so how did the unemployment happen in the first place? And that is an excellent question.

One of the things about the simple description of entropy and entropic forces is that it requires that there's no biases or correlations in the distributions of the large number of things from which the force emerges. If all the cream became frightened of your mouth, the cream might suddenly sink to the bottom of the coffee cup. In that case the entropy would spontaneously drop. That's a violation of the famous second law of thermodynamics: entropy never decreases on average in a closed system. Another way to phrase it is to say heat flows from hot to cold. Now cream doesn't become frightened and panic, but people do. Financial markets can suddenly be overcome with a wave of pessimism that leads to falling prices and — if it goes on long enough — a panic. A market sell-off is a correlation of people's pessimism. If it was a system of molecules, we'd see the entropy drop. It also means that a drop in entropy could be overcome with coordinated action. For example, the government could just hire a bunch of people — like it did with the Works Progress Administration (WPA) during the Great Depression. So if we can apply the concept of entropy to economics, it's a different kind of entropy from a different kind of thermodynamics that doesn't have a second law — something more like the abstract entropy in information theory. However, before we get to that I want to tell another story about the relationship between microeconomics and macroeconomics.

SMDH

In the 1970s, around the same time as the push for microfoundations, came a series of results from mathematical economists Hugo Sonnenschein, Rolf Mantel and Gerard Debreu that should have put a damper on that push. They found (loosely speaking) that many different sets of assumptions about individuals in an economic model could lead to the same overall economy. It's called the SMD theorem after Sonnenschein, Mantel and Debreu.

There are some other implications as well. One is that there could be many different equilibrium states for the overall economy: high unemployment and low unemployment, low inflation and high inflation, low unemployment and low inflation, *et cetera*. Two, each of those equilibrium states can be considered unique if you don't move very far away from them.

Let's say a blueberry has a few properties: its color, its plumpness, its flavor, and its size. The SMD theorem would be like proving that a blueberry pie (the economy at large) only inherits the color and flavor from the individual blueberries. Berries of different sizes and plumpness, but the same color and flavor would lead to the same blueberry pie.

It seems that most economists who paid attention to the SMD theorem immediately tried to get around it. A popular way was with a representative blueberry. If there was just one big blueberry, then the blueberry pie would be the same color, flavor, size and plumpness of that blueberry.

Of course, if you have one representative agent in the economy, that raises some questions: How does that representative agent make deals with itself? How can you have a situation where there are two different forecasts for the future in one representative agent's mind such that the agent both wants to sell a stock and buy it? If there's a transaction, there's always a buyer and a seller. That's hard to reconcile with only a single representative agent. But the representative agent allowed economists to keep human agency at the center of macroeconomics.

The other implications of the SMD theorem say that the blueberries could end up as a blueberry smoothie or blueberry pancakes (multiple equilibrium states), but these are locally unique -- small changes from a blueberry pie is still a blueberry pie and not a blueberry smoothie.

For me, the most interesting implication of the SMD theorem is that the idea of what a blueberry is simplifies (for example, only color and flavor) near a macro equilibrium whether that macro equilibrium is a blueberry pie, a blueberry smoothie or blueberry pancakes.

This hits on a basic principle of physics: theories tend to simplify near an equilibrium. Even complex quantum field theories look a bit like a pendulum (a generic oscillator) near an equilibrium. One way this can manifest is through what physicists call new effective degrees of freedom. The theory becomes a theory of different things from that which it consists of fundamentally. We know that a superconductor fundamentally is made of atoms consisting of nuclei (which are themselves made of quarks and gluons) and electrons, but we describe a superconductor with Cooper pairs of electrons, not single electrons. The fundamental particle content and the effective particle content (also referred to using the adjective "dressed") aren't necessarily the same. Actually, this is where I differ from a common criticism of economics: that rational agents aren't realistic descriptions of people. We all know that economies are fundamentally made up of people. However, near an equilibrium, economies might be made of rational agents. This simplification of the agent-content of the theory might fail away from equilibrium — or might never be true in the first place. It is not *a priori* silly to make economies out of rational agents, though.

It may well be that these simpler explanations *must* exist at different theory scales (under different scope conditions). Neuroscientist Erik Hoel wrote a paper "When the Map Is Better Than the Territory" in 2017 expounding on the theory of "causal emergence". Using a novel information theory argument from an earlier paper he co-authored, Hoel showed that better (less lossy in the presence of real world noise) causal explanations could exist at various scales. Those causal explanations of natural systems are like communication signal demodulators (decoder) for nature, however one decoder only works on data with a specific "modulation" (encoder). A causal description in terms of atoms is one modulation; a causal description in terms of humans is another. The atomic modulation works well for a lot of physical systems where effects at the atomic scale matter (the microscale), but the human modulation is probably better for describing macroscale economies and societies (an atomic description of GDP is almost certainly intractable). Rational agents might be an even better decoder than realistic humans at the scale of a macroeconomy near equilibrium. Hoel's argument doesn't tell us what these effective "agents" are at the various microscales or macroscales, but it does tell us it is probably hard (i.e. lossy) to describe a macroscale system using microscale agents. Additionally, it opens up the possibility that new emergent "agents" may be necessary to describe the macroscale.

Consider a macroeconomic state space with multiple stable equilibria (say a high growth economy and a low growth economy). Generally, the fundamental theory that describes both equilibria is complex. However, in the neighborhood of a stable equilibrium (say the high growth economy), the theory simplifies with new effective degrees of freedom — for example: optimizing agents with rational expectations. It is important to remember that these effective descriptions are tightly linked with the scale at which they appear and the scope conditions implied by the assumptions involved.

One way to interpret this is that rational agents are a fiction — the true microfoundations are the microscopic theory underlying the locations of the two equilibria. A second way to interpret this is that it is possible we have an effective theory of rational agents when we are near equilibrium — and that these effective theories might be different near different equilibria.

The question I'd like to ask is whether we can consider Gary Becker's irrational agents to be an effective theory near our observed macroeconomic state? Can we forego rational representative agents and relying on theories of human agency?

The economic problem

Could it be that the problem with economics is that it does not question the idea of human agency? If the major principles of economics don't give results that differ from random agents that don't look to the future, what holds up? That really pulls the rug out from under the traditional approach to economics. Or does it? Here's Adam Smith in the *Wealth of Nations*:

> *[Every individual] is in this, as in many other cases, led by an invisible hand to promote an end which was no part of his intention.*

Adam Smith was talking about the merits of restricting imports, but it may be the "many other cases" that has led to the ubiquity of the invisible hand. The end of that sentence may be our key: "no part of his intention". Maybe economic agents just randomly (or at least randomly to an outside observer) explore the opportunity set and it's the changes in the bulk properties of the opportunity set that give us the invisible hand? In this view, the invisible hand is an entropic force that has to do with the probability of being in a particular state in the state space. The invisible hand doesn't exist for individual agents any more than diffusion exists for individual atoms. This view has consequences for how we should look at the price system.

While the invisible hand is one of the longest lasting insights of economics, another long-lasting insight is Friedrich Hayek's argument that the prices in markets aggregate private knowledge. Hayek uses the word "information" in the original, but I'd like to replace it with "knowledge" in order to keep the technical term information — a measure of bits or bytes — separate. Here's Hayek in "The Use of Knowledge in Society" (1945):

> We must look at the price system as such a mechanism for communicating [knowledge] if we want to understand its real function — a function which, of course, it fulfills less perfectly as prices grow more rigid. (Even when quoted prices have become quite rigid, however, the forces which would operate through changes in price still operate to a considerable extent through changes in the other terms of the contract.) The most significant fact about this system is the economy of knowledge with which it operates, or how little the individual participants need to know in order to be able to take the right action. In abbreviated form, by a kind of symbol, only the most essential information is passed on and passed on only to those concerned. It is more than a metaphor to describe the price system as a kind of machinery for registering change, or a system of telecommunications which enables individual producers to watch merely the movement of a few pointers, as an engineer might watch the hands of

> *a few dials, in order to adjust their activities to changes of which they may never know more than is reflected in the price movement.*

This has been a pervasive insight, but I'd like to try and convince you that it is wrong. First let me tell you how it is understood.

Let's say there is a hard freeze and this season's crop of blueberries is devastated. What happens? As we have all seen, the grocery store wastes no time in raising the price. According to Hayek, the knowledge of a freeze has been communicated through the price. Similarly the knowledge of a bumper crop is supposedly communicated to us consumers via a fall in the price of blueberries.

How does this look as a real communication system, though? Imagine all the blueberry farmers and all the blueberry consumers are in a meeting room, on a speaker phone. Everyone is talking about how many blueberries they'd like at one price and how many are available at another. A classic market. All of the discussion — all of this knowledge — is picked up by the speaker phone. On the other end of the phone line is just a light that gets brighter or dimmer. That's the analogy of the price going up and down.

So the question is: Do you think you could back out what is being said on the other end by just looking at the light flickering? Like the cream mixing in the coffee and the probability distributions leading to a normal distribution in the central limit theorem, there are an infinite number of discussions on the other end that could lead to a particular brightness.

Now it would be possible to somehow set up a system like Morse code that communicated what people were saying, but it would take much longer to encode and transmit than for people to say it (and the farmers and consumers are talking at the same time). It is clear that the knowledge is being smashed into the price, not communicated by it.

Joseph Stiglitz, economist and Nobel laureate recognized this; he writes in "The contributions of the economics of information to twentieth century economics" in 2000:

> *The exchange process is intertwined with the process of selection over hidden characteristics and the process of providing incentives for hidden behaviors.*

Those hidden characteristics and behaviors are part of the infinite number of discussions on the other end of the speaker phone. Stiglitz is saying no one-dimensional price could possibly capture the multidimensional processes that lead to that price.

One thing to bring up here is that the work in

information asymmetry and information economics Stiglitz is known for should really be called "knowledge asymmetry" and "knowledge economics" because the "information" is meaningful. George Akerlof's 1970 article called "The Market for Lemons" described the case where the seller of a used car had more knowledge about the state of that used car than buyers — "information" asymmetry. It is way too late to undo the unfortunate naming of this useful insight, but it really should be called knowledge asymmetry. That the seller knows more meaningful facts about the car — the specific bit sequence placing it the state space of cars — is more salient than the number of bits required to place the car somewhere in the state space of cars — the information represented by selecting a car out of that state space.

I try to keep track of the difference between "knowledge" and "information" because we are now talking about channel coding and a subject called information theory, developed by a mathematician and engineer at Bell Labs named Claude Shannon in the 1940s. Shannon's insight was that information in the technical sense is different from meaningful knowledge — in fact, for information in information theory, we don't really care about the meaning. Information theory is sometimes made to seem to spring fully formed from Shannon's head like Athena, but it has some precursors in Ralph Hartley's and Harry Nyquist's work on transmitting signals and Morse code via telegraph. Both even worked at Bell labs.

Information is usually measured in bits (a one/zero or on/off state). There are eight bits in a byte and a one gigabyte flash drive can store about one billion bytes of information. Note that it doesn't matter whether there are picture files or documents on the drive — the meaning of the bits is irrelevant to the quantity of information that can be stored.

Now a bit is the amount of information you get from a selection of a one or a zero from a set that has a one and a zero in it. We can call that selection an "information event". A common example is that a bit is the amount of information you learn when you find out whether a coin has come up heads or tails: a selection of heads or tails from set (coin) that has a heads and a tails side. A flip of a coin is an information event.

You don't have to stick to coins and bits, however. Selecting letters out of the Latin alphabet also is information. Specifying a capital letter requires about 4.7 to 4.8 bits (depending on whether you include spaces). And the string of letters:

BILLION

requires about 33 bits to specify out of the alphabet. This is another good example where information isn't meaning: that word means different things in French (1,000,000,000,000) and American English (1,000,000,000). The meanings are different, but it is roughly the same amount of information.

The informational equivalence is not exact because certain letter combinations more commonly occur in a given language. For example, a Q is almost always followed by a U in English, so given a Q, the U contains almost no information. But it's good enough for our purposes.

As you can see, information is intimately related to probability. With this in our mind, we have another way to think about economics. We can think of the case where supply meets demand and markets "clear" as cases where demand information events meet supply information events (together comprising a transaction information event). Equilibrium happens when the distribution of demand events is matched by the distribution of supply events. This better aligns with the communication channel picture: in equilibrium (i.e. communication is happening) the demand events on one end of the communication channel are all matched up with supply events on the other end — much like the letters in a text message on my cell phone matching up with the letters received on your cell phone. We can call this matched up condition *information equilibrium*.

Peter Fielitz and Guenter Borchardt derived an equation in their 2011 paper "A generalized concept of information transfer" that represents a condition that must hold in information equilibrium. Interestingly, the equation that results from matching up the information content of these probability distributions is almost identical to one economist Irving Fisher wrote down in his PhD thesis "Mathematical Investigations in the Theory of Value and Prices" in 1892. On the next line, Fisher inserts a utility function, but the basic argument involving bushels of one commodity and gallons of another is there (Fisher doesn't say what the gallons and bushels represent). He attributes the argument to the English economists Alfred Marshall and William Jevons. Marshall is credited with inventing the ubiquitous supply and demand diagrams (although various diagrammatic methods had existed before). Jevons was a key figure in the so-called marginal revolution (marginal utility) and, according to Fisher, was one of the originators of using math in economics.

Going back to our speakerphone analogy, now we consider the consumers on one end of the phone line and blueberry farmers on the other. People are yelling out bids (I'll pay two dollars for a pint) on one side and asks (I'll sell a pint for three dollars) on the other. When these balance, you could say the volume (loudness) on each speaker is about the same. When you get an imbalance, there will be more asks or more bids (i.e. more information), making one side louder than the other. When this happens in real markets, the market price goes up or down.

Price is therefore a measurement of the imbalance between supply and demand information events. A higher price for blueberries just tells us supply is low or demand is high. As an aside, there is an interesting formal similarity between this picture and Generative Adversarial Networks (GANs) — an algorithm developed in 2014 used in unsupervised machine learning: the demand information is the real data, the supply information is the machine-generated version, and the price is the so-called discriminator.

I think this is important to understand the difference here. The price mechanism isn't solving a *knowledge* problem as Hayek hypothesized — telling us of a freeze damaging the blueberry crop; it is solving an *allocation* problem — matching blueberry consumers (demand events) with blueberry farmers (supply events). Like the machine learning GANs, we are matching the information in the allocations of supply and demand.

Note this is where using information for both knowledge and in the information theory sense would get us in trouble because that sentence written confusing the two would say that the price mechanism isn't solving an information problem; it is solving an information problem. We could clarify it a bit by saying the price mechanism isn't solving an information aggregation problem; it is solving an information allocation problem.

Now for a long time, economists assumed that under ideal conditions the allocation problem was exactly solved by ideal markets. This lead to the view that unemployment (unallocated workers) was simply due to a lack of desire to have a job whether due to unemployment insurance or too high reservation wages (how much workers think they should be paid). The Great Recession of 2008-9 was sarcastically called the Great Vacation by opponents of this view. The idea that unemployment could persist was the primary motivation for the hypotheses in Keynes' *General Theory*.

A different hypothesis called the non-accelerating inflation rate of unemployment (NAIRU) was also developed to explain unemployment and inflation. In this view, the fewer people that were unemployed led to greater competition for workers, which resulted in higher wages. These higher wages would lead to a wage-price spiral (since people had more money, they could afford more stuff, meaning demand was higher, so prices were higher) and accelerating inflation. It was hypothesized that at some level of unemployment, inflation would be constant. Sometimes this is talked about as the natural rate of unemployment, analogous to the natural rate of interest where a similar dynamic with inflation happens.

These are all still a neoclassical models: the markets are working, they just don't employ everyone for rational reasons.

More recently, economists have looked to Dale Mortensen's (and others') matching theory, which can be thought of as a relaxation of the solution to the allocation problem. Matching each additional person with a job costs more (in search costs on both the employer and applicant sides), so that at some level it costs too much to find a job. When you reach that point, you've reached a natural rate of unemployment.

Information equilibrium represents an even more relaxed solution of the allocation problem. In information equilibrium, we only consider the probability of job opening event and a job application event (forming a hire event) to be high. A large number of people in the work force (millions) means that the law of large numbers kicks in and the real world distribution of hire events is closely approximated the probability distribution of hire events.

Instead of supply and demand perfectly meeting, or partially meeting, we just say there is a high probability of supply and demand meeting in equilibrium. Additionally, because you can only receive as much information as was sent, this matching of probabilities is the best you can do. Having too many blueberries (supply events) at one grocery store is as big of a problem as too few at another; having too many demand events for blueberries at one grocery store is as big of a problem as too few at another. The different events "bunch up" in the available opportunity sets. This can be temporary (and corrected by the market), or it can be chronic — leading to fewer demand events meeting supply events and lower overall sales of blueberries.

The information theory picture separates these two kinds of disequilibrium. In our speakerphone analogy, the first case occurs when you have a crystal clear connection. Everyone can hear and understand everyone on either end, but there is a temporary imbalance in blueberries supplied by farmers and demanded by buyers. In the second case, there is either noise on the line so that some transactions don't occur or possibly the language used for communication isn't the first language of either the farmers or the buyers (for example one side speaks Arabic, the other French, and they are communicating in English). I remember a real world example of this from a linguistics class back in college. One trader was trying to tell another that the cheese he'd sent was "blowing" in customs which the other trader didn't understand — until it looked like he was going to lose money. At which point the two found a common phrase ("gone off") and he recognized the cheese was spoiled.

This brings us back to Gary Becker's model. We are looking at the information flowing back and forth to keep the probability distributions of supply events and demand events in the opportunity set in equilibrium. As long as information equilibrium holds — for example, the agents choose opportunities in the opportunity set uniformly and don't bunch up, economics is the study of properties of the opportunity set. But what happens when this fails? That's the question I address next, and provide a speculative answer.

Economics versus sociology

What happens when information equilibrium and assumptions about assigning equal probability to each opportunity in the opportunity set break down? Let me try an example that is based on a bee hive.

The bees represent economic agents, and the observed dances and other behaviors are the social theory of the agents. The bulk properties of the hive (size of cells, size of hive, honey output) represent the economic theory. We can tell some things by appealing to the law of large numbers. The size of a cell varies a bit, but the average size (for a given species) can be pretty well known. The number of bees gives us a good estimate of the size of the hive. These give us a good idea of honey output regardless of the individual dances telling us the direction to some blueberry flowers with tasty nectar. Large scale coordinations break down these relationships (e.g. a swarm to find a new home).

Most of the time — when there isn't large scale coordination, when the bees don't bunch up in the opportunity set — there is a separation between the social theory of the bees (the particular way they find nectar, the hierarchy of a hive) and the economic theory of the bees (the production of honey). My hypothesis is that when this separation holds, then economics is more like physics. When it doesn't, economics is more like sociology.

If the details of the complexity of bee social structure and the messages they communicate to each other strongly mattered, it would (likely) be impossible to figure out how much honey you could get from 50,000 bees (roughly the size of a hive). But there are typical amounts (about 50 pounds in a season). Now humans are more complicated than bees, but the same principle — that the macro properties are mostly governed by the bulk properties of the available state space – has to apply if macro is tractable. And if it's not tractable (a possibility), then economics really should just reduce to moral and historical arguments.

The key point is that (probably) the only way the actions of millions of complex humans can be aggregated and understood in a tractable way is for something like entropy and entropic forces to kick in. In that case, the bulk properties of the state space tell us more about macroeconomic properties than the properties of the agents. Also in that case, as long as the social science of the agents meets some pretty general constraints, there is a separation between the economics (study of the state space) and the social science (study of the agents). The tractable mathematical laws of economics are emergent and (somewhat) independent of the social agent substrate.

I think this is the lesson of the SMD theorem. Sure, complex agent models could be used to understand economics, but so can simple random agent models with uniform distributions over the opportunity set. In fact, lots of different agent models (micro theories) likely map to the same macroeconomy. When considering honey production, bees lose a lot of their details much like blueberries lose a lot of their details when they are part of a blueberry pie.

When the details of bee societies matter, honey production ceases to be an economic question and becomes a bee sociology question. Honey production is reduced when a hive swarms instead of supersedure (where a new queen takes over for the old queen). These actions can be coordinated by dances or pheromones. In a similar way, the economy is under the purview of economics when the details of economic agents (humans) don't matter. When the details of human behavior matter — for example, through politics or the panicked selling accompanying a stock market crash — the economy is under the purview of sociology. It is possible that economists don't understand what recessions are yet because they have the wrong tools — recessions are not explainable using bulk properties of the opportunity set and the approximately rational agents that exist in equilibrium.

This puts economics in a position of straddling two very different domains. At one end of the spectrum, we have a human. They are unpredictable; understanding a human is tantamount to producing artificial intelligence. The fields of psychology and neuroscience aim to understand how our human brains work, and sociology aims to understand how humans interact. At the other end of the spectrum, we have an aggregate ecosystem on a planetary scale. On this end, we have physics, geology, chemistry, ecology and biology.

On one side, we have aggregates that do not depend strongly on their constituent agents. Water and carbon cycles can be understood in terms of very general thermodynamic processes (or even entropy production). The planet and its ecosystems can be understood in terms of generic predators and prey, available food energy, and evolutionary niches. Ecosystems can be understood without knowing why the chameleon evolved its color changing abilities. We can guess that desert creatures will be brown. This is not to say everything can be explained simply, but resource constraints and evolution are powerful principles that get answers that are close to being right.

On the other side, we have aggregates that strongly depend on their individual agents. A brain is more than just a lump of neurons. Different kinds of animals form different hierarchies. Human societies have vastly different social norms that appear to be important in macroeconomic outcomes. You can't guess how a brain will behave given a neuron and you can't guess how a society is structured given a human.

In the middle is economics. There are certain aggregate properties we believe hold across economies — like the economic forces of supply and demand. But there are aggregate properties that economists try to show are the result of specific individual choices and incentives. Economics is sometimes a hard science and sometimes sociology. Unless there is something very different at the mesoscale, this means that hard science will encroach on its aggregate findings on one side and sociology, psychology and neuroscience will encroach on its human-centric findings on the other.

This creates an ironic situation. While economists are touchy about physicists encroaching on their turf (recall our discussion of Chris House earlier), they seem perfectly fine encroaching on psychology and sociology (one of Gary Becker's aims). Economists claim that sociology should use math better, less obscure jargon, and be more empirical. This is the essence of this physicist's complaint about economics!

I do want to emphasize again that this is speculative. I'd like to leave these as open questions.

I quoted Keynes in the chapter where I laid out my critique:

> *In the long run we are all dead. Economists set themselves too easy, too useless a task, if in tempestuous seasons they can only tell us, that when the storm is long past, the ocean is flat again.*

Is it possible that economics is the study of that flat ocean? Does it simply lack the tools to address the tempestuous seasons? That would make sense of the lack of consensus on what a recession is as well as claims to be unable to predict recessions. *The Telegraph* reported on November 5, 2008 that Queen Elizabeth II asked academics from the London School of Economics "Why did nobody notice it?" in reference to the financial crisis. Maybe the cause had more to do with us as humans than us as economic agents? Maybe the question should have been asked of sociologists at Oxford?

Are we not agents?

At this point the idea that economics — when it works — might be the random trial and error of mindless agents usually runs into its last bastion of resistance. Isn't it obvious that humans are intelligent beings making plans and thinking strategically? This has been such an obvious starting point that even in the days of the proto-economists (the so-called physiocrats of the 18th century), there was discussion of the impacts of "anticipations" of government policies on markets. Game theory arose as a field of mathematics to codify and understand strategic thinking that quickly found a home in economics departments. Everyone can probably recall a recent trip to the grocery store where they weighed the prices of different products in order to try and save money.

The random trial and error (the economic term is *tâtonnement*) in entropy maximization does not preclude these things from happening. In fact, there may even be a direct connection between entropy maximization and intelligence. In a paper titled "Causal Entropic Forces" (2013), Alex Wissner-Gross and Cameron Freer propose exactly that:

... no formal physical relationship between intelligence and entropy maximization has yet been established. In this Letter, we explicitly propose a first step toward such a relationship in the form of a causal generalization of entropic forces that we show can spontaneously induce remarkably sophisticated behaviors associated with the human "cognitive niche," including tool use and social cooperation, in simple physical systems. Our results suggest a potentially general thermodynamic model of adaptive behavior as a non-equilibrium process in open systems.

In the description of Wissner-Gross's November 2013 TED talk on the subject, the result of this paper is called "an equation for intelligence". The authors simulate simple systems that can demonstrate tool use and social cooperation based on causal entropic forces. The "causal" here just means a restriction of the state space to states that are accessible at a given time given a particular starting point (in physics, the initial condition). For example, if it takes a long time (say a day) to go from A (the starting point) to B, then B is not is not an accessible position state for time periods shorter than a day. The probability of being in state B should be zero until a day has passed. Note that this is the exact same causality that is violated by rational expectations where the future state B influences the present state A as we discussed earlier. But in the causal entropy formulation, it is just the lack of access to B in the present that influences the present state A.

In an example in economics, that state space could be the opportunity set and the causal volume (the opportunities available) could be bounded by income. I could have to wait until my next paycheck to save up $50 in order to access the state of owning 10 pints of blueberries (at $5 apiece) in order to make jam. A causal entropic force could push me towards using my credit card — or even humans inventing credit as an economic tool in the first place. Finance itself could be considered the process by which we humans gain access previously inaccessible opportunities in order to maximize causal entropy. Stocks originally were designed to spread risk and enable companies to pool money together. That allows the company to find states that individual humans thought too risky and cost too much money. Banks "borrow short" and "lend long" — an opportunity not available (at low enough risk) to individual agents with limited horizons.

The key point here is not that our human intelligence is unimportant, but rather that it might be unnecessary to understand how economic systems work … at least when they work. Causal entropy maximizing but mindless agents could perform all the same tasks as rational utility maximizing agents. The difference is that in the former case the properties of the state space (dimension, symmetry, and now causal structure) are the driving factors, not the properties of the agents. If that is true, economic systems potentially become tractable — dependent on the tens of parameters describing the state space rather than the millions of agents. Our human agency and complexity is reduced to an assumption of fully exploring the economic state space.

However, as discussed in the previous chapter, the entropy picture fails when humans fail to explore the entire state space and their actions start to correlate. And when that happens, the properties of millions of agents becomes more important than the tens of parameters describing the state space. A financial crisis might be too complex to model or even understand using economic theory. It might not even be consistent with the actions of intelligent agents, but rather depend on psychology and neuroscience. And if entropy maximization is related to intelligence, then is this why herd behavior and panicking in markets appears unintelligent from an economic perspective?

Conclusions

What should economists make of all this? First, I think they should use random agent models as a good test to determine whether the conclusions they draw from their experiments and models are showing us agent behavior or properties of the state space. Read or re-read Gary Becker's 1962 paper. Try to think of humans as so complex and inscrutable that they appear totally random. This viewpoint sets up a framework where the equilibrium solutions are no longer perceived to be the optimum of some subjective "good" measure like utility (and therefore deviations are "bad"), but simply the most likely state. Just because the equilibrium we observe is likely doesn't mean some other less likely state is better or worse.

Second, economics should consider itself a nascent field. Even though it has been over 200 years since Adam Smith wrote the *Wealth of Nations*, the total of the widely applicable consensus theoretical knowledge explaining empirical data that has accumulated would probably fill a few pages. I guess the standard model of physics can be written on a t-shirt, so that isn't necessarily a criticism if taken in isolation. However from studying the subject for several years the only experimentally or statistically validated "truths" appear to be supply and demand and Okun's law (a direct relationship between output and employment). And the former only "works sometimes" (in particular, not in labor markets), with little discussion of the scope of the theory in elementary or advanced textbooks to tell us what "sometimes" means.

That might be a bit of an exaggeration, but it is not meant as an insult! Economics is hard, with enormous data and measurement difficulties as compared to any science. And yet it is so important we cannot give up. It means it's an exciting time for economics. There was a time in physics when all we really had to go on was Huygen's principle and Galilean invariance. I see the opportunity for a future Isaac Newton, Emmy Noether or Charles Darwin of economics to completely change the way we think about the field.

Third, economists should assume expectations at infinity (or the distant future) have no dependence on the actual future. This is both mathematically sensible as well as practical. Our beliefs of the future are exactly that: beliefs.

The physicist Lee Smolin suggested in his 2009 preprint "Time and symmetry in models of economic markets" that what is needed is an approach that is capable of dealing with non-equilibrium situations that he called "statistical economics" by analogy to statistical mechanics in physics. I think Gary Becker's work on the rationality of irrational agents was a step in this direction, and I hope my work using information equilibrium turns out to be a positive contribution — although I admit it might turn out to be the wrong path. That is exactly the issue. No one knows yet what is right or wrong in economics. It is in the state physics was before Isaac Newton produced its first coherent framework.

What should the rest of us make of all this? The main lesson I hope to impart is that the ruthless (or robotic or idealized) view of human behavior that the dismal science takes isn't the only way to explain the world of money. It has garnered the name *Homo economicus* as a play on our species' name *Homo sapiens*. We're not necessarily out to get the best deal without regard to others — we could well be random explorers of an abstract numerical universe. It's also odd to subscribe to that dim view of greedy efficiency when it doesn't necessarily result in understanding that abstract numerical universe any better! And it seems especially odd to me that we ask economists' advice on money, inflation, or recessions when there's no consensus economic theory that explains any of them.

Additionally, we should prize the colorful members of our society — the ones that think differently. They are the ones exploring the new parts of the social and economic state space. We should give them a safety net for when they explore too far. The thing is, all of us are a special recombination of our parents' DNA — we all bring a unique hue to the crayon box. We can all explore that state space. And the maximum entropy way to cover that state space is with a uniform distribution. The Nordic countries come the closest to this "theoretical" ideal, but total redistribution hasn't been achieved on any national scale.

While a uniform distribution is unlikely — and may not be ideal because sometimes the motivation to explore parts of the state space is money — there is probably some middle ground that is optimal from a political perspective. Personally, I don't think someone pursuing money as a goal in itself is going to find it to be very fulfilling. But everyone's preferences (within reason) deserve non-zero weight in our collective objective function. In policy circles and even among some economists (including even Milton Friedman), there is support for the idea of a universal basic income. The idea is that no matter what you do with your life, you should at least get enough money to live. This seems like a good compromise between the uniform distribution and political reality. Of course, exploring can turn up negative things for other explorers. Economists call these negative externalities and they should be mitigated — whether it be dumping carbon dioxide in the atmosphere or a bank taking on so much leverage that it threatens the global economy.

Another thing is that everyone doing their part to select products is providing a valuable service to businesses. Distributing money so that everyone can select products makes products better. Remember that economists think competition is good — that competition requires as many people to participate in it as possible.

However, the biggest lesson I'd like people to take away is one that economists already understand well. Our economic world is not zero-sum. As mentioned in the glossary, zero-sum is a term of art in the game theory mathematics used in economics. It means the gains of one person are the losses of another (i.e. the total gains and the total losses by everyone add up to zero). However, your exploration of the economic state space is valuable to you *and* me. Increasing the number of agents exploring that space is valuable to the agents already exploring it. As we saw in the chapter on comparative advantage, trade benefits *both* nations engaging in it. Redistribution of wealth is beneficial to both those who end up transmitting *and* those that end up receiving wealth. And if economic forces are emergent entropic forces then the concepts of economic gain or loss do not even exist if you only observe at the scale of individuals.

We should also avoid pretending knowledge where it does not yet exist. There is nothing wrong with starting from a state of ignorance and saying "I don't know."

Acknowledgments

I'd like to take the opportunity to thank several people. Many thanks to David Glasner for pointing me to Gary Becker's 1962 paper which has proved to be both an invaluable resource for insight into how economists think as well as a "cold open" for introducing my ideas to economists . Thanks to Brennan Peterson and Cameron Murray for volunteering to edit/read the manuscript. Thanks to Tom Brown, a frequent commenter on my blog, for asking questions that helped me clarify the ideas presented here.

But most of all, I'd like to thank my wife Nadgia and my step-daughter for being such lovable weirdos dedicated to fully exploring the state space together despite the fact that I have been hunched over in front of a computer deep in economic research over the past few years or travelling extensively for work.

I'd also like to dedicate this book to my father, Ray Smith, who passed away in the summer of 2016. He was my model for endless curiosity and exploring every field. My interest in economics grew out of our frequent political arguments and discussions, and he was the one who told me about Keith Chen *et al*'s paper about capuchin monkeys. I will miss him.

Made in the USA
Columbia, SC
31 August 2017